Studies in Irish, British and Australian Relations, 1916–1963

‘The bright day, runs towards the night, night leads on to dawn’

Margherita Guidacci, 1988
Translation by Anne and Catherine O’Brien

Studies in Irish, British and Australian Relations, 1916–1963

Trade, diplomacy and politics

Collected essays by John B. O'Brien

Anne E. O'Brien
EDITOR

FOUR COURTS PRESS

Set in 11 on 14 Ehrhardt for
FOUR COURTS PRESS LTD
7 Malpas Street, Dublin 8, Ireland
email: info@four-courts-press.ie
http://www.four-courts-press.ie
and in North America by
FOUR COURTS PRESS
c/o ISBS, 920 N.E. 58th Avenue, Suite 300, Portland, OR 97213.

ISBN 1-85182-881-8

A catalogue record for this title
is available from the British Library.

Printed in England
by MPG Books, Bodmin, Cornwall.

Contents

Abbreviations

AA	Australian Archives
NAI	National Archives of Ireland, Dublin
NLA	National Library of Australia, Canberra
PRO	Public Records Office, Kew, London [National Archives]
SPO	State Papers Office

Acknowledgements

There are many people who have helped with the publication of this volume and who have supported the project in its various stages. To all of them I extend my deepest thanks: Professor J.J. Lee, Professor Dermot Keogh and Professor Tadhg Foley who were unfailing in their support; Four Courts Press for their work on this book and for agreeing to take on the project; Larry Geary, Mary White, Tom Silk, David Fitzpatrick and Tom Dunne, thank you all for your special contribution. I would also like to express my appreciation to the following for allowing me reprint certain articles: *Historical Studies*, *Irish-Australian Studies*, *Journal of the Cork Historical and Archaeological Society*, *Round Table*, Colm Kiernan, Alex May and F.B. Smith (eds) *Working Papers in Australian Studies*, YHI.

Lastly, this collection would not have been published without Professor Catherine O'Brien's belief in the project, her hard work and faith in its realisation. Hopefully this book will be a worthy testament to her late husband, John B. O'Brien.

The photograph of John O'Brien, used as the frontispiece of this book, was taken in the Barossa Valley, South Australia, 27 September 1998.

Anne O'Brien

SPECIAL ACKNOWLEDGEMENT

Publication of this volume has been made possible by generous grants from the NUI Publication Funds and the Arts Faculty, University College, Cork.

John O'Brien, 1938–1999: an appreciation

John Bosco O'Brien, being an Irishman, hovered between various worlds. Home was always Munster, particularly the Golden Vale. He was born in Thurles, Co. Tipperary, on 15 December 1938; grandfather O'Brien had farmed near Galbally, Co. Limerick; and after 1970, when he took up a Statutory Lectureship in History at University College, Cork, he spent as much time as possible at a farmhouse that he acquired at Lissard (signifying High Fort) near Galbally. His father was born on the farm, but moved to Thurles and set up an electrical business after marrying a local draper.[1] When John wrote about agricultural prices, rural banks, or the Catholic middle classes, he had the advantage over most economic historians of personal experience.[2] In Dublin, he liked to impersonate a canny Munster farmer enjoying the fleshpots of the metropolis, whether in the University Club or the hostelries of Baggot Street. I recall many happy reunions leading up to an Irish-Australian History conference held in April 1987, when he and I were members of a wonderfully disorganised organising committee under the benevolent aegis of the late Reverend Professor F.X. Martin, OSA.[3] The residual Kildare Streeters at adjoining tables in the University Club must have been perplexed by these lunchtime meetings, where the elegant Augustinian would reminisce about his visits to the Soviet Union and the down-at-heel countryman would unveil himself as a cosmopolitan scholar. In Cork, the academic persona tended to prevail, and his postgraduate students at University College remem-

1 Rosa O'Brien died on 27 August 1980, a decade after her son's return to Ireland, and Joe followed her three summers later, on 25 August 1983. I am most grateful to Catherine O'Brien, now Professor of Italian at University College, Galway, for answering my queries about John's background and early career and for her invaluable comments on the text. 2 'Agricultural Prices and Living Costs in Pre-Famine Cork', in *Journal of the Cork Historical and Archaeological Society*, lxxxii, no. 235 (1977), pp 1–10; 'Sadleir's Bank', in ibid., pp 33–8; *The Catholic middle class in pre-Famine Cork* (Dublin, 1980). 3 The other organisers were Pauric Travers, now President of St Patrick's College, Drumcondra, and Bob Reece, now Director of the Centre for Irish Studies at Murdoch University, Perth (when on secondment as Keith Cameron Professor of Australian History at University College, Dublin). Most of the conference papers were published as John O'Brien and Pauric Travers (eds), *The Irish emigrant experience in Australia* (Dublin, 1991).

bered him as a hard task-master and a constructive but relentless supervisor. Yet his irreverent humour and warmth soon erased any impression of severity among those who attended his supervisions or classes.[4] At Lissard, which I visited in 1972 when it was barely fit for human habitation, the academic was transformed into a Trollopian gentleman of the old Gaelic stock, fallen upon hard times, as an ancient retainer served up the best (that is, worst) done bacon and cabbage I had ever tasted. Prudently, we had already eaten before embarking on what turned out to be a leisurely journey from Cork, mainly in second gear, as we stalked some pack of hounds pursuing their hapless quarry across the nearby fields. The object of John's stealthy scrutiny was not a horse, hound, or fox but one of the hunters, a lecturer in Italian at UCC named Catherine Cooke. Before long they were wedded in what would once have been deemed a 'good match' (her father had a farm not far from Galbally). He was clearly besotted with Catherine and their five children, who provided him with an essential anchor and recreated his Irish home.

Yet, as John Henry Newman ruminated in the celebrated Anglo-Catholic hymn that introduced John's Requiem Mass on 4 March 1999:

> I was not ever thus, nor prayed that Thou
>   Shouldst lead me on;
> I loved to choose and see my path; but now
>   Lead Thou me on.
> I loved the garish day, and, spite of fears
> Pride ruled my will: remember not past years.

My strongest memories of John O'Brien relate to his other world which, though never quite 'home', dwelt in his imagination to the end – Australia. After graduating from University College, Dublin, in 1960, and mastering at Manchester University two years later, he had moved to Australia in 1963 to take up a research post with the Commonwealth Bureau of Census and Statistics. His first academic post (in 1965) was in Adelaide, where the late Oliver MacDonagh had recently moved from Cambridge to become Professor of History at the new Flinders University of South Australia. Though John worked in the more conventional environment of Adelaide University, MacDonagh soon became a close friend as well as an academic mentor. His exemplary studies of the Passenger Acts and Guinness's Brewery probably stimulated John's interests in the broader ramifications of administrative and business his-

4 'Dr John B. O'Brien: historian. An appreciation', in *Decies*, no. 56 (2000), pp 213–14.

tory.[5] MacDonagh rehabilitated the humanitarian element as a factor in explaining bureaucratic decisions, and showed that the records of a single company could give practical meaning to the notoriously vague idea of 'modernization'. MacDonagh also set an example of how to organize an academic career straddling Ireland and Australia, but proved hard to keep up with. Scarcely had John reached Adelaide before MacDonagh left for Cork, where he presided over Modern History for six years before re-migrating to Canberra in 1973 as Professor of History at the Australian National University's Institute of Advanced Studies. John, having followed him to Cork three years earlier, was again left stranded in the wrong hemisphere. The link survived these disruptions, as MacDonagh constantly revisited Ireland (sending his sons to Clongowes) while John in later years made almost annual pilgrimages to Australia. MacDonagh outlived his protégé, dying in Sydney in 2002 at the age of 78.

I came to know John O'Brien as an undergraduate at Melbourne University, where he encouraged my perverse wish to work on Irish Nationalism, then regarded by most at Melbourne as a tragi-comic footnote to British and Imperial history. He had recently been appointed to a lectureship at La Trobe University in uttermost Melbourne, where he developed another lifelong friendship and academic affinity with the late Allan Martin. Martin, who later joined MacDonagh in Canberra and wrote a superbly crafted life of Sir Robert Menzies, was not only a punctilious scholar and fine writer but a warm and sensitive personality unsuited to La Trobe's crass faculty-fights. Together, in 1969, they took the risk of appointing a very raw Bachelor of Arts (Hons.) without any relevant experience to a full-time tutorship. My 'interview' (I was the only candidate) occurred over coffee at an outdoor table in one of the tree-studded expanses of the new campus, where concrete and glass blocks were erupting everywhere. My task each week was to take eight tutorial groups on the same topic in the already legendary History 1A, a compulsory Humanities course covering every notable element of the twentieth-century world – except Britain. Three weeks were devoted to Ireland, and John was the course director. Along with Ron Fitzgerald, a liberal-minded Catholic and an influential educational reformer who believed in keeping his hand in by teaching undergraduates part-time, we plotted ways of shocking our motley crew of 'mature' students and semi-literate but often bright children of immigrants into arguing about Communism, Fascism, and above all Irish Nationalism. Since there

5 Oliver MacDonagh, *A pattern of government growth, 1800–60: the Passenger Acts and their enforcement* (London, 1961); S.R. Dennison and Oliver MacDonagh, *Guinness, 1886–1939: from incorporation to the Second World War* (Cork, 1998). Notoriously, publication of the latter work was delayed for over a quarter of a century following objections by the company.

were several other teachers in this vast course, including the radio quiz-champion and solicitor Barry Jones (later Australia's Minister for Science), we sometimes found ourselves locked in pedagogical battles, which all added to the fun. In these debates, John O'Brien always took the sterner side, stressing the need for academic rigour and objective assessment while neglecting no device capable of distracting students from their usual preoccupations.

Each Tuesday night, John, Ron, and myself would visit a sprawling suburban 'hotel' for a strategic discussion, a few beers, and a massive plate of lightly garnished cholestorol, leaving the seminar rooms unlocked and each group under the control of a chairman charged with getting discussion underway. By the time we had driven back to Bundoora, say twenty minutes late, impassioned arguments would often be audible as we swayed down the corridor. Our task was to sit back, listen, take notes, and, as a last resort, intervene. Afterwards, a student who had been teaching all day in a primary school would sometimes take me aside and offer sage words of advice and encouragement on my 'teaching'. By about 9.30 p.m. we were ready to disperse, allowing time for a return dash to the pub before last orders to discuss the evening's classes, the attributes of the students, and the next step in our struggle against the opposing faction with its soft and sloppy approach to assessment. These evenings supplied my only useful training as a university teacher. They also showed O'Brien the mentor at his best, enabling me (like the students) to learn my trade through experiment and debate rather than submission to instruction.

The same approach was applied to learning how to lecture, potentially an intimidating prospect with several hundred first-years expecting an intellectual entertainment rather than today's string of plagiarized bullet-points. We tutors were invited but not required to attend lectures by the grown-ups, and likewise to deliver lectures in fields removed as far as possible from our own (if any). My own initiation included three lectures on international diplomacy and the Spanish Civil War. When I ran out of material early in the third lecture and declared open house, the debate became so heated that I had to be saved from the vengeance of student Trotskyites by a plain-clothed Sister of Mercy, who gently deprecated my Stalinist tendencies but would defend to the death my right to express them. In those heady days of seemingly limitless funding for new universities with a mission to educate 'the masses', La Trobe had been able to secure luminaries of international renown and (by Melbourne standards) irresistible eccentricity – notably Israel Getzler, the biographer of Martov. Even in such company, John was an acknowledged star, using his wit and broguish charm to seduce audiences of half-Australianized Greeks, Italians, Serbs, and Croats into appreciating the ironies and absurdities of history. As he got into his stride, this would become increasingly erratic. Students gasped as he paced across the podium, teetering over the brink to make a point, once walking through a glass exit to the rather callous delight of the class. The dramatic impact of his teaching technique in Australia was of course heightened by John's exoticism, but something of the old elixir of zest and precision survived his return to Ireland. During his first term in Cork, he wrote to me that he had 'introduced some of the La Trobe 1A tutorial techniques with apparent success (chairmen etc.). The students were a bit aghast initially but are now taking them in their stride – in fact the tutors here are also adopting them!'[6]

John O'Brien had more to teach us than how to teach or learn history. In Australia, he seemed to embody Ireland, keeping in touch with home through a host of informants plus the indispensable Tipperary Star, which arrived each week from his mother in Thurles. He radiated a notion of Ireland which was at once hard-headed and mysterious, promising insights into murky depths of Irish life that remained taboo among historians and even journalists. Then as now, Irish religion and politics offered rich pickings for connoisseurs of hypocrisy. John briefly joined the North-East Ireland Relief Committee, Melbourne's counterpart to Noraid, before resigning in disgust after establishing the true destination of funds raised on behalf of a certain 'Widow McGuinness' (or somesuch) and her seven orphans, whose dolorous plight had emptied the pockets of so many compassionate Australians. His often scurrilous depiction of Republicanism and its manipulation of 'the risen people' during that emotive period was a useful corrective to Australian incomprehension of Irish issues and to my own latent sentimentalism. Despite his strong Catholic convictions and close friendship with intellectual priests, particularly Jesuits and Augustinians, he relished passing on folklore about incest, bigamy, clerical abuse, and other signs that all was not as it seemed in pious Ireland. John was a truth-teller, whose hints about concealed realities goaded one into asking awkward questions and ferreting out relevant evidence. This characteristic may have been more warmly welcomed in Melbourne than in Cork.

He returned to Ireland in style, preferring the leisurely luxury of the Marconi to the frenetic discomfort of an aeroplane:

> The trip over was good fun – the Italian service was superb and the company congenial. There was a small number of young ones and what was lost in quantity was adequately compensated by the quality. There

6 Letter to author, 6 Nov. 1970. Certain words, inscribed in O'Brien's inimitable scrawl, may have been misread.

> were a number of randy unallotted [?] married women whom I stayed clear of but for anyone inclined in that direction they could have passed the trip without seeing the light of day!

This first letter to me reads exactly as I remember him speaking:

> Ireland hasn't changed much . . . Some facilities have been modernised though overall I'd say the prevailing attitude is as it was. While everybody is interested in and respectful of money the majority are not inclined to exert themselves in acquiring it and seem more bent on spending what little they have. I was at the races in Listowel the other day – mid week – and there were as many present as at Flemington on a Saturday with money and beer flowing freely. We had a repetition [?] the other night of a theatre protest. During a review satirising Northern Ireland a scuffle broke out and the protesters ranted from the stage – as is typical, one of the female objectors recited poetry in front of the stage lights. I've bought myself a car – a Ford Capri, and so far it's going smoothly – I've only got one slight dent in it.[7]

Cars, races, money, and beer all fuelled his joie-de-vivre in Ireland as in Australia (though he looked after his investments more attentively than his cars). Another diversion was hockey, the only form of strenuous exercise in which I ever knew him to indulge. We had sometimes lined up for La Trobe, John darting down the wing while I lumbered about the back line. I last watched him play in September 1977, still exuding bravado as he lunged in the general direction of the ball.

John's approach to historical research was another matter. In an unpublished lecture delivered in Waterford in the mid 1990s, he expressed an already unfashionable determination to seek 'the truth' by applying 'facts' in the pursuit of 'causation, coherence and generalization'.[8] While admitting that all historical explanations are contestable and shaped by the context of writing, he affirmed the need for professionalism, adequate documentation, and analytic rigour. This led to the rather pessimistic reflection that historians, being subject to the 'tastes of contemporary society' with its imperatives of 'relevancy, immediacy and functionalism', were bound by their traditional responsiveness to the market 'to supply the types of studies demanded'. He was referring to that oxy-

7 Letter to author, 29 Sept. 1970. 8 'The nature of history': typescript kindly supplied by Anne O'Brien.

moron 'contemporary history', a genre which he regarded as 'a pale approximation of authentic history', marred by defective documentation and unavoidable shallowness of perspective. He was equally scathing about the alternative popular taste for compilations of 'colourful anecdotes' that 'masqueraded as history', yet were 'invariably devoured by the general public in the belief that they are imbibing the genuine article'. By confining his own work to old-fashioned analysis of testable questions, John clearly felt himself to be at odds with both the historical profession and the reading public. Perhaps he yearned for those long obsolete 'goals of progress, self-improvement or even scientific certainty', which had shaped and animated the great nineteenth-century histories. Caught in the prosaic present, he could scarcely be expected to find a theme or topic capable of fully expressing his deepest preoccupations.

Though he never published a book, John O'Brien made significant contributions to Irish, Australian, and British Imperial history. He served intermittently on the committee of the Economic and Social History Society of Ireland, and published several brief but thoroughly documented studies in the economic history of Cork, occasionally venturing as far as Tipperary. He worked hard to raise the standard of research in local history, especially through the Cork Historical and Archaeological Society. Yet he spoke of himself as an Australian rather than an Irish specialist, introduced the teaching of Australian history to Irish undergraduates, and became Treasurer of the European Association for Studies of Australia.[9] His first major Australian study was a doctoral thesis, completed in Cork in 1972, on the Melbourne Steamship Company. Like the company itself, the topic ended up going nowhere. The resultant book was on the very point of publication in Australia when a bushfire destroyed the entire stock. John had neglected to keep a copy of the corrected proofs, and no phoenix emerged from the ashes. Instead of pursuing business history, he embarked on a series of articles and papers which collectively display his varied perspectives on Ireland and Australia. Originally published in a medley of journals and conference proceedings, some of these have now been edited by his daughter Anne and brought together in this book. The effect is to conjure up his keen interest in Irishness and Catholicism in Australia, demonstrate the force of his comparative approach to administrative and economic history, and suggest the books that might have been.

9 Joe Lee, 'Valete: John O'Brien and Graham Little', in Philip Bull, Frances Delvin-Glass, and Helen Doyle (eds), *Ireland and Australia, 1798–1998* (Sydney, 2000), pp. 343–8.

The first four chapters explore some of the complexities of Australia's Irish and Catholic histories, amplifying rather than challenging the pioneering work of the late Patrick O'Farrell in both fields. Much emphasis is placed on the wider repercussions of personal shortcomings in prompting historical change. The startling transformation of Daniel Mannix (Archbishop of Melbourne, 1917–63) from cautious Home Ruler to Republican hero is attributed primarily to his misguided demonisation by the Conscriptionist Prime Minister, W.M. Hughes. The effect of Hughes's paranoia, fanned by the split in his ruling Labor Party, was to undermine Irish-Catholic support for Home Rule and the War effort, exacerbate the existing sectarian animosities, and greatly strengthen Mannix's political influence. Likewise, the abrasive manner of Archbishop John Panico (Apostolic Delegate to Australasia, 1935–48), retarded the 'Australianization' of the Church by enabling Irish vested interests to focus their opposition to his reforms on matters of personality rather than principle. These studies undermine the facile assumptions, still sometimes uttered, that the Catholic Church in Australia was inherently Irish, and that 'the Irish' were intrinsically anti-Imperialist.

The remaining chapters illuminate the chequered economic history of the British Empire during its protracted decline into a British Commonwealth and subsequently a mere Commonwealth of Nations. For British governments after the Great War, the Dominions were an economic encumbrance, whose reiterated demands for preferential tariffs threatened Britain's trade with the wider world and particularly, from the 1960s, with continental Europe. This factor was somewhat mitigated by the political prestige derived from maintaining the appearance of an Empire, and by the genuine desire of the Dominions Office to maintain close relations with Australia and, if possible, even with Ireland. As O'Brien shows, mutual misjudgments were critical in undermining the economic efficiency of the Commonwealth as a trading bloc. Successive Australian governments and High Commissioners over-estimated the influence of their allies in the Dominions Office, and failed to sustain Australia's apparent triumph in Ottawa at the Imperial Economic Conference of 1932. According to O'Brien's elegant analysis, Australia's success at Ottawa was partly due to the mistaken British hope that de Valera's new Irish Government could be enticed to seek an accommodation with the hereditary enemy. These hopes were subverted by de Valera's stubborn refusal to embrace the apparent advantages of defensive association with the Commonwealth during the Great Depression, or to recognise the erosion of British dominion over the 'Dominions'. Indifference to the Commonwealth fostered ignorance of British intentions and attitudes, painfully evident in 1948 when de Valera's opponents, in government under Costello, risked catastrophic penalties by their abrupt decision to repeal the External Relations Act without warning the Dominions in advance. Attlee's Cabinet, initially free from pressure by allies such as Australia for yet another Irish compromise, interpreted the break with the Crown as an opportunity to define 'Éire' as a foreign power which would no longer enjoy preferential trade or rights of residence for its citizens in the United Kingdom. Only the unexpected (and unexplained) intervention of Dr Herbert Vere Evatt, Australia's Minister for External Affairs, persuaded Britain to salvage something from the mess by bestowing 'dual citizenship' on the seceders. Just as the Irish factor had fostered Australian interests in 1932, so an Australian initiative rescued Ireland from its own diplomatic folly in 1948.

John O'Brien, as many of these chapters show, was at his best when showing the historical impact of personal failings, misjudgments, and unpredictable changes of attitude. Using an ever broader range of official and private archives, initially British but later also Australian, he was adept at documenting key personal exchanges and setting these firmly in political and administrative context. Except in broad surveys such as the first and final chapters, he avoided speculative arguments and ringing conclusions. His keen sense of the absurd was mostly kept under control, apart from occasional sardonic asides. Yet, even in the most disciplined essays on administrative history there are personal resonances, as in those accounts of chance intersections between Irish and Australian interests. Our last reunion, only a few months before his death, occurred appropriately at La Trobe University during yet another Irish-Australian conference. His delivery of the paper appearing here as the second chapter showed that he had lost none of his old zest and capacity to engage an audience. Later, at the conference dinner, he became wonderfully merry and led me from table to table recounting tales of our Melbourne past to all and sundry. This book does belated justice to the achievement of a generous man and a good scholar, whose seemingly disjointed research interests were unified by the patterns of his own life.

David Fitzpatrick
Trinity College, Dublin

I

The Irish in Australia, 1945–1968

One of the most remarkable features of the Irish in Australia is the way in which they preserved their identity for so long. While it had been the ultimate aim of nations with immigrants to merge all groups, ethnic or otherwise, into a discernible new milieu, the Irish in Australia resisted any such move for close on 150 years, thereby retaining their traditional characteristics and forming a sub-culture within Australian society. Even though the Irish shared many of the features of the dominant Anglo-Australian establishment, such as colour, language and even physical appearance, their attachment to their Irish traditions, particularly to the Catholic religion, their support for separatist movements in Ireland and the reinvigorating effect of fresh waves of Irish immigrants, kept them apart. Being at least 25% of the population also helped. They could not be absorbed against their own wishes.

On the other hand, the Irish in Australia were never large enough to create another Ireland in the Southern hemisphere. While they preserved such Irish values as a concern for family life, loyalty to the Catholic Church and, to a lesser extent, Irish songs and games, they were never in a position to impose these on the rest of society. They remained outside the dominant Anglo-Australian establishment. The resistance of the latter to Irish assimilation was equally important in ensuring the preservation of a distinct Irish identity in Australia. Based on a long legacy of animosity and suspicion, the attitude of Anglo-Australians served only to reinforce in a negative way unique Irish features. For example, the strength of Anglo-Australian resistance to Irish Catholicism tended on many occasions, to intensify its importance for the Australian Irish, while Anglo-Australian condemnation of the Fenian and Home Rule movements and their support for British repression in Ireland, further alienated Irish-Australians. As a result, the Irish in Australia and those of Irish descent were still a clearly visible ethnic minority as late as 1920 despite the fact that the number of Irish immigrants to Australia had been declining for many years.

As a pressure group, Irish-Australians achieved little for themselves: they failed to obtain state aid for their Catholic schools, they failed to gain support for, or even to interest Anglo-Australian politicians in the Home Rule movement, nor did they succeed in inspiring much general interest in Irish games, songs or dances. Until recently the thought of an Australian republic was anathema to most non-Irish-Australians. The Irish in Australia were least successful in matters that were more or less idiosyncratic to themselves. On the other hand, they could be quite effective when they moved out of their own ethnic enclave to pursue targets of a more general kind. Because of their coherence, they could tip the balance. Their support was often sought by groups wishing to challenge the Anglo-Australian establishment in such matters as land reform or constitutional change. In that way, the Irish in Australia played an important role in forging distinctive Australian social and political institutions. These were not Irish: they mostly conformed to the specifications of the dominant Anglo-Australian majority; but the Irish did have an impact.

In the process, it became quite clear, especially to the more politicised of the Irish, that in Australia they had more to gain from cooperation with the Anglo-Australians than from opposition. While that might entail a certain loss of identity, it nevertheless guaranteed a say in the political process. With the formation of labour parties in the 1890s, the Irish found an acceptable vehicle for their political ambitions: but even though the Irish were very well represented with nearly 40% of the parliamentary party of Irish extraction between 1920 and 1960, they still failed to write any peculiarly Irish policies into the parties' platform. There have been three Australian Labor Party prime ministers of Irish extraction, James Scullen, John Curtin and Joseph Benedict Chifley, none of whom supported state aid for Catholic schools or were more actively involved in Irish affairs, such as Northern Ireland, than their Liberal Party counterparts. Irish-Australians in politics became less Irish and more Australian and the Australia which they projected was until quite recently, an Anglo-Saxon version.

That version had been jealously guarded by the Anglo-Australians primarily because it confirmed their privileged position at all levels of society but also because it conformed to their concept of the ideal Australia: a country loyal to the monarch, predominantly Protestant, committed to the empire and a safeguarder of British democratic traditions. As long as the Catholic Church in Australia was ministered by Irish born and Irish trained clerics and while Irish-Australians actively supported separatist movements back home and large numbers of Irish immigrants continued to arrive, Anglo-Australians feared for their own heritage and seemed to over-react at the slightest challenge. Irish participation in politics was one such threat. So entrenched had the dominant ethos become by the time the Irish made political headway that they found it impossible to make any real impact. In fact, it was the Irish-Australian political activists who had to make the change. As a result, the price of success either in politics, business or the professions very often entailed a dilution of their own Irish heritage and placed a barrier between the successful Irish person and his fellow countrymen. After 150 years in Australia, the vast majority of Irish-Australians were excluded from the sources of real power and influence. They had maintained their identity; but that was of greater significance for themselves than for Australia.

Then came the Second World War and as a result a remarkable transformation in Australian perceptions took place. The Japanese attack exposed the vulnerability of Australia to possible invasion and to the danger of its vast territories being over-run by millions of Asians. Australia found that it had insufficient people now that it desperately needed them. Birth rates in the 1930s which had fallen to an all-time low, coupled with wartime mortality, meant that Australia could not rely on her own resources for an increase in her population. Australia had to look elsewhere, initially to Britain and Ireland, then to northern Europe, followed by Southern Europe and as a last resort to selected pockets in Asia. An immigration programme designed to augment the population by 1% per annum through migration was launched shortly after the war.

As a result, the most dramatic feature of Australian society during the next twenty-five years was the change which occurred in its composition: from being a predominantly Anglo-Saxon Irish society, it became a cosmopolitan one, embracing immigrants from most European countries, east and west and in recent years, it also admitted immigrants from Asia. Between 1947 and 1964, more migrants were added to the population than in the eighty years since 1860.[1] As a result, the proportion of those born in Ireland has been substantially reduced. In 1901, 21.4% of emigrants to Australia were Irish-born. By 1947, this figure had fallen to 6%; by 1954 it was 3.7%; in 1961 it was 2.8%; and by 1970 it was only 2.5%.[2] By that year, there were three times as many Italian migrants living in Australia as Irish; the number of Poles about equalled the Irish while, most surprisingly of all, the number of Asian-born Australians was almost double that of Irish-born Australians.[3] These developments had a profound effect not only on the character of Australian society, but also on the situation of the Irish. From being the largest minority group, the Irish now found themselves in a minority within the minorities. As a consequence, their presence was scarcely perceptible. For example, in official figures, the Irish were

1 Geoffrey Blainey, *The tyranny of distance* (1966) p. 334. 2 Charles A. Price (ed.), *Australian immigration* (1971), pp. A78, A79. 3 Ibid.

invariably coupled with the British and the British Isles cited as the origin of both British and Irish migrants. Officially, at least the British and Irish had become a homogeneous group.

Faced with such a large intake of migrants, Australia had to decide how it was going to absorb them. Her initial response to this challenge was to insist that the New Australians, as they were termed, conformed to the standards, modes of living and aspirations of traditional Australia just as the Irish had earlier been expected to conform to Anglo-Australian precepts, before being accepted. A homogeneous Australian way of life was enunciated, which tended to ignore the cultural traditions of the new migrants. Australia was not yet ready to risk the impact of diversity, even if there was a strong likelihood of it being enriched in the process. As in the past, cultural variations were viewed as an affront to a society that demanded social uniformity; but the big difference on this occasion was that the Australian-Irish were now party to the plot.

This was because the Irish were now viewed as constituting the least likely danger to the plans of the dominant majority. In the face of the threat from New Australians, any ally was welcome, even if it meant setting aside over 150 years of history. But of importance too was the added factor of the Irish-Australians becoming more acceptable in their own right. To begin with, they were more affluent than hitherto; they were less obviously Irish Catholic; they appeared to have lost interest in Irish affairs and, of course, there were fewer of them arriving.

Unlike the United States, where the middle classes had been decisive from the beginning, Australia began with a dominant upper class and a large working class with little in between. A pastoral ascendancy which was predominantly Protestant, dominated the politics, economy and society of the young colonies. In the twentieth century industrialisation augmented the ranks of the Australian middle classes, among whom were included many of Irish descent. The Irish were now no longer at the bottom of the social ladder: a survey in Melbourne in 1965 found that almost 50% of the unskilled labour force were migrants and 27% were persons born in southern Europe.[4] The 1954 census revealed that only 15.8% of all Australian born males were employed in manufacturing compared with 23% of north-west Europeans, 37% of central and eastern Europeans and 31% of southern Europeans. Comparable figures for the building and construction industries were: Australasian born 6%, north-west Europeans 15%, central and eastern Europeans 12% and southern Europeans 12%.[5] Each of these ethnic groups were also under-represented in com-

4 I.H. Burnley (ed.), *Urbanization in Australia* (1974), p. 181. 5 R.T. Appleyard, 'The population'

merce (that is compared with Australian born) and with the exception of southern Europeans they were also under-represented in agriculture. The Irish could now afford the trappings which constituted the Australian way of life of the 1950s and 1960s. These entailed a home in the suburbs, a car, a television set and a style of life which laid more emphasis on material than on cultural accomplishments.

Australia was merely participating in a world-wide trend that had its origins primarily in the United States. It is doubtful if Australia's participation would have been as wholehearted twenty years earlier. Disenchantment with Britain for its neglect during the Second World War and a recognition of the vital role played by the United States in the Pacific war pushed Australia closer to the latter. This was later institutionalised within the Anzus Treaty. At the popular level, the connection was strengthened by the advent of television in 1956, which in its early years depended largely on United States productions. A gallop poll in 1958 found that only 29% of voters thought that the United States was influencing the Australian way of life too much.[6] The British stranglehold on Australian perceptions and values was being eroded and as a result Irish-Australians found cultural assimilation much more palatable.

The rapid increase in the number of Catholics in Australia after the war from approximately 17.5% of the population in 1933 to 26% in 1968,[7] also had a profound effect on the status of Irish Australians. As the principal reason for this increase was the large influx of southern Europeans, a dramatic change took place in the composition of the Catholic community in Australia. Catholics and Irish were now no longer synonymous. The Irish-Australians could still be distinguished in the practice of their religion. A survey in 1971 found that 56% of Irish-Australians attended church at least once a week in contrast to 30% of southern European born Catholics and 42% of other Catholic migrants.[8] This loyalty to their religion was now conditioned by two developments, one recent and the other stretching further back. Firstly, the ecumenical spirit of the 1950s and 1960s meant that Christians of all denominations were less abrasive and were less antagonistic towards one another. Secondly, by the 1960s, the Australian Catholic Church came to be dominated by an Australian trained clergy. It was indeed a coincidence that the latter's spiritual message, while pre-dating the ecumenical age, was scarcely discernible from it.

in A.F. Davies and S. Encel (eds), *Australian society* (1965), p. 13. 6 Richard White, *Inventing Australia* (1981), p. 162. 7 Patrick O'Farrell, *The Catholic Church in Australia* (1968), p. 275. 8 Burnley, *Urbanization in Australia*, p. 188.

Since the foundation of St Patrick's Seminary in Manly in 1889 by Cardinal Moran, for the training of Australian-born priests, the aim was to Australianise the Catholic Church in Australia, to make it self-reliant and to ensure that its relations with its flock and the environment were based on indigenous values. Whilst not for a moment denying the inestimable contribution made by Ireland to Catholicism in Australia, the Manly products believed they should now devote their efforts to rooting out secularism and materialism in Australia, rather than concentrating exclusively on the converted, or shadow boxing with Protestants. In this respect, they shared many of the concerns of the other Christian churches, which were also most disturbed by the growing numbers of religiously indifferent in Australia. The Australian-trained clergy also believed that their response to the religious needs of Australia required a flexibility in outlook which in their opinion was less forthcoming from those trained in the more restrictive atmosphere of Irish seminaries. What they wanted was an Australian clergy for an Australian Catholic Church. 'Just as the Irish had argued in the nineteenth century in opposition to English Benedictines that a predominantly Irish laity needed a predominantly Irish priesthood so Australian priests were arguing that a predominantly Australian laity needed an Australian priesthood.'[9]

By the 1960s, the majority of the Australian clergy were Australian born and by the 1970s only a few Irish-born bishops remained and those mainly because of longevity. The success of the Australian priests meant that while Irish-Australian Catholics remained loyal to their Catholic heritage, they could no longer be accused of merely echoing the dictates of Irish seminarians. As a result, they became more acceptable to the Anglo-Australian majority. The most tangible expression of this has been the concession in 1964 of state aid to denominational schools by Sir Robert Menzies, a Liberal Party prime minister.

From being almost totally committed to a solution of Irish political problems, by the 1960s Irish Australians had become at least indifferent to them. Many who had given active support during the Anglo-Irish War were disgusted by the Civil War and so began to distance themselves from their former homeland. There was little to enthuse them in the Ireland of the 1920s, 1930s and 1940s and even when in 1948 Mr de Valera arrived in person to rally support against partition, his reception was tepid. Irish-Australians had become more and more concerned with Australia and the drop in the number of Irish immigrants over the last fifty years meant that now there was less chance of the

9 O'Farrell, *The Catholic Church in Australia*, p. 247.

old flame being rekindled. As a result, the last remaining barriers between themselves and the Anglo-Australian majority were being dismantled.

It should therefore be evident that by the 1960s the Irish in Australia had been culturally assimilated into Australian society. They identified more with Australia than with Ireland; they shared most of the characteristics and aspirations of their fellow Anglo-Australians: they were clearly distinguishable from the new Australians who now had to tread the same road that had taken the Irish more than one hundred and fifty years to traverse. All that now remained was for the Anglo-Australians to accept them as equals within the establishment itself. This entailed entry to their clubs, to their businesses, to their political parties, where they would be taken into confidence and advantageous contacts made. The process here had, however, been relatively slow: whereas Irish cultural assimilation was under the control of the ethnic group itself, this structural assimilation as it is termed by sociologists was at the exclusive discretion of the host society.

A few instances of the exclusiveness which still persists give a good indication of the hesitancy of the establishment to open its ranks: the Liberal Party and its non-Labor precursors have been the preserve of the Protestant Anglo-Saxon Australian establishment since the very foundation of Australia. Even in 1958, only seven out of the one hundred and eight members of the parliamentary Liberal Party were of Irish extraction, though that was an improvement on 1922 when the comparable figure was only three. In 1961, nearly 28% of Catholics, most of whom were of Irish extraction, indicated their intention of voting Liberal;[10] but this was not translated at the polls into the return of a proportional number of Irish-Australian members. They still depended on the Australian Labor Party for that endorsement. The medical and legal professions have traditionally been monopolised by Anglo-Australians but while this has not deterred the Irish-Australians from entering these professions it has meant that a higher proportion of the latter has been forced into public employment because of limited scope in private practice. The attorney general's department and the registrar general's department have been noticeably popular with Irish-Australian lawyers.[11]

With no entry restrictions in the public service, it is understandable that Irish-Australians should have been especially attracted to it, so that a higher than average proportion of civil servants have been of Catholic Irish extraction. The Catholic population of Canberra has been significantly higher in post-war

10 S. Encel, *Equality and authority* (1970), p. 166. 11 Ibid., p. 285.

years that the national urban average of Catholics. Professor Encel suggests that the proportion of Catholics in the civil service in Canberra may be as high as 40%.[12] In these respects, the public service has provided a stepping stone on the path of Irish structural assimilation. Irish-Australians also encountered similar discrimination in business: membership of exclusive clubs like the Adelaide Club, the Melbourne Club and the Queensland Club has been mainly confined to the Protestant Anglo-Australian establishment. In fact in Queensland, the Labor premier in 1956, Mr Vince Gair, found it necessary to pass an act giving the victims of black-balling the right to appeal to a court.[13] It is interesting that his conservative successor promptly repealed that act. While full structural assimilation has not yet taken place, instances of discrimination have been rare in recent years. Whereas the stock exchanges excluded Irish Catholics in the past, both the Sydney and the Melbourne exchanges now admit them. For New Australians, less attuned to the nuances of discrimination, Irish-Australians were hardly distinguishable from the dominant Anglo majority. As far as they are concerned the Irish in Australia have arrived.

But had they arrived too late and did they pay too high a price for their assimilation? Measured against the Australian way of life of the 1950s and 1960s, which emphasised suburban Australia with its materialistic values and hedonistic pursuits, it is quite obvious that these were poor substitutes for the cultural diversity of their discarded Irish heritage. The Irish had cast aside their ethnic anchorage in exchange for an homogenised Australian identity – the Wild Colonial Boy was now a nine-to-five worker. But the real irony was that, having sacrificed so much, the reward was so ephemeral. It may well be, as Andrew Greeley observed about the Irish in the United States, that their counterparts in Australian stopped 'being Irish the day before it became all right to be Irish'. The WASPS won the battle to convert the Irish into WASPS just before the announcement came that a permanent peace had been made with diversity.[14]

By the end of the 1960s the racial exclusiveness and the intolerance of the 1950s was giving way to a multi-cultural pluralist society in Australia. This was due to a number of factors. It was almost inevitable that after acclimatising themselves to their new environment the New Australians would begin to assert their own identities and then, because of their numbers and their concentration, it was likely that they would breach the prevailing orthodoxy. Secondly, Australian participation in the Vietnam War led to a crisis in Australian society because of the widespread opposition to government policy. Finally, the inter-

12 Ibid., p. 284. 13 Encel, *Equality and authority*, p. 133. 14 Andrew Greeley, *That most distressful nation* (1973), p. 263.

national youth culture of the 1960s, with its lack of respect for conventions, its questioning of accepted standards and its outrageous behaviour in speech, dress and life styles, began to percolate into Australia and to undermine belief in their way of life. Irish-Australians now found that the society to which they had aspired for so long and within which they had only recently been recognised as equals, was about to undergo a remarkable metamorphosis. From being a monolithic Anglo-Saxon and latterly Irish society, it was to burst forth into a pluralist one.

A new role was found for the aborigines, who were now encouraged to develop their traditional crafts and skills and to preserve their customs and rituals. No longer were they herded into ghettos and forced to conform. Dents were also made in the White Australia policy, with the admittance of a limited number of non-Europeans. In short, the parameters of Australian life were extended latterly to embrace a wide range of life styles and customs. But these parameters have also been extended vertically in an effort to refine the Australian identity in response to the questions being generated by the changed mood of the late 1960s and early 1970s. For example, the dramatic growth in the number of overseas arrivals has stimulated interest in demographic change, in the history of migration and in the place of minorities in Australian society.

As the largest and oldest minority, the Irish have obviously been the focus of much attention. This has led in the past ten years to a blossoming of Irish ballads, Irish dancing, Irish games and Irish clubs. Irish history is now being taught at universities not as an adjunct to British history, but rather for its own sake. It is now possible to be a good Australian and still retain one's interest in one's own cultural heritage. And so the stage has been reached where the Irish in Australia no longer have to struggle for acceptance or make cultural sacrifices for the sake of assimilation. The changed character of Australian society and the new climate means that at last it is possible to be both a good Australian and proud at the same time of having Irish origins.

2

The Irish revolutionary movement and W.M. Hughes, 1916–1922

In his lengthy account of the Australian Prime Minister, William Morris Hughes, in the *Australian Dictionary of Biography*,[1] Laurie Fitzhardinge makes no reference to Ireland while, in his monumental biography of Hughes, he alludes to Irish Australians in only sixteen of his 670 pages,[2] suggesting that Irish affairs were a cursory intrusion in Hughes's career. Hughes himself would have questioned that judgment: in a letter to Lloyd George in August 1917, he complained that 'the Irish question is at the bottom of all our difficulties'. Commenting on the Wharf Labourers' strike of that year, he stated that 'they – the Irish – have captured the political machinery of the Labour organisations [. . .] and are mainly responsible for the trouble',[3] while he also attributed his defeat in the 1916 conscription referendum to the fact that the Catholic Church was 'secretly against recruiting. Its influence killed conscription.'[4] In a letter to Keith Murdoch, destined for Lloyd George, he further alleged that the 'bulk of the Irish people, led by Archbishop Mannix are attacking me with a venomous personal campaign', and there are other pertinent references.[5]

Fitzhardinge was well aware of these protestations by Hughes but, for the most part, he deftly sidestepped them, thereby implying that Hughes may have exaggerated their significance. However, while Hughes may have been mistaken in the weight which he attributed to his perceptions of Irish machinations, there can be little doubt that the consequences of these developments, in particular Hughes's own misinformed responses, contributed substantially to Australian divisions between 1919 and 1921.

Hughes had a very limited, even simplistic knowledge of Ireland, the Irish and of Irish affairs, which is surprising considering his Welsh antecedents, his upbringing in Wales itself, his long association with the Australian Labor Party,

1 *Australian dictionary of biography*, vol. 2. 2 L.F. Fitzhardinge, *W.M Hughes: a political biography*, vol. 2 (1979). 3 Hughes to D. Lloyd George, 17 August 1917, quoted in Fitzhardinge, *W.M. Hughes*, p. 276. 4 Ibid. 5 Murdoch to Lloyd George, 29 April 1917, quoted in Fitzhardinge, *W.M. Hughes*, p. 286.

his presence in Wales on Easter Monday 1916, albeit suffering from one of his many peptic bouts, and his long sojourn in London in 1918 and 1919, at the height of the convulsive upheavals in Anglo-Irish relations. Still, on none of these occasions is there any evidence of him displaying even the remotest interest in these developments, not to mention involvement in their resolution, unlike, for example, Menzies during his brief visit to Ireland in 1936 or Evatt's chance presence in Dublin in 1948. Hughes's priorities then and subsequently were quintessentially Australian; his role on the world stage was strictly confined to the pursuit of Australian interests and, while he did dominate much of the Versailles proceedings, he never went beyond his Australian brief. His 1916 sojourn in England was confined to the War Cabinet and to Australian trade: the Easter Rising was an irrelevancy.

He could be excused for ignoring recent Irish upheavals. The Australia which he left behind in January 1916 was still harmonious: he had observed in 1914 that 'the gravest crisis in our history is faced by a united people',[6] while John Gavan Duffy speaking, as he said himself, as an Irish Catholic nationalist, noted that

> in this crisis Irish Nationalists forgot all grievances of the past. Justice is being done to them at the present time and they were ready, eager and willing to stand shoulder to shoulder, knee to knee fighting the battle of the Great Empire.[7]

The justice which was being done to them was the introduction of the 1912 Home Rule bill, the realisation of all Australian-Irish aspirations. Home Rule, as Patrick O'Farrell has so elegantly observed, 'seemed to be the vehicle on which those Irish Australians together with the Irish in Ireland would ride with comfort into the warm welcoming heart of the Empire'.[8] Ireland, like Australia, would become a free country within the British Empire.[9] John Donovan, William Redmond and Richard Hazeton, who visited Australia in 1912, all testified to the absence of rancour there; Donovan reported that 'the change is remarkable. Take the Envoys meeting in Melbourne and Sydney. You had there all the leading politicians and the distinguished ecclesiastics . . . of all denominations.'[10]

On the eve of the Easter Rising in March 1916, the St Patrick's Day procession halted outside the Federal Parliament in Melbourne while 'God save the

6 W.M. Hughes, 9 August 1914. 7 Quoted in E. Scott, *Australia during the War*, vol. 11 (1936), p. 24. 8 Patrick O'Farrell, *The Irish in Australia* (1987), p. 250. 9 Ibid., p. 259. 10 *Melbourne Advocate*, 12 October 1912.

King' was played. The Home Rule solution suited Irish Australians admirably. They could reconcile without difficulty their old and new loyalties. They could be loyal to Ireland, Australia and the Empire simultaneously, without any conflict. Thus, the Irish Catholic community was as heavily committed to the war as any other sector in Australia: sons of prominent Irish-Australian Home Rulers such as Dr McCarthy, Dr O'Donnell, Thomas Fogarty and Morgan Jaguers all enlisted early on. John David Jaguers was killed at Gallipoli; a stained-glass window in St Mary's Cathedral in Sydney commemorated second Lieutenant Brendan Mullins, killed in action in France in June 1917;[11] while seven Irish-Australian VCs led the St Patrick's Day parade in 1920. But by its very nature this sense of unity was conditional – conditional on the ultimate achievement of Home Rule – in that sense it owed little to the therapeutic dollops of Gallipoli and elsewhere provided by Ashmead-Bartlett, Macefield or Bean.

The imperial dimension for most was conditional on the Irish and it is most likely that Hughes failed to recognise that fact. The jingoistic beat further impaired his already deficient hearing. It was only later that Hughes recognised that the Home Rule card was the one to play but by then it was too late. By overemphasising, on his return in August, the imperial dimension other than the purely Australian one, while the Irish-Australian consensus was fragmenting, Hughes helped to create a situation which he had actually sought to avoid, that is a society polarised along sectarian lines. Modern research has shown that this defeat in the first conscription referendum in October 1916 was not due to Irish Catholic opposition – it may have shaded the outcome in particular areas – but a combination of traditional Labor hostility, concern for civil liberties and an economic dimension had a far greater impact. The Easter Rising did not lead to a gush of Anglophobic sentiment in Australia – anti-imperial sentiment was slow to emerge and even then, for many Irish Australians, it was camouflaged in pro-Australian protestations. For example, Mannix himself regarded the Rebellion as 'truly deplorable', 'lamentable' and its leaders 'misguided'.[12] Other ecclesiastics were even more voluble. Clune of Perth considered it 'insane' and Carr of Melbourne 'an outburst of madness, an anachronism',[13] and 'a crime against the Irish Parliamentary Party'.[14] From all over Australia, Irish nationalist groups sent cables to Redmond, and even to Prime Minister Asquith, pledging their loyalty. 'Sectional, pro-German rioting disgusts Home Rulers here', reported the New South Wales Home Rule executive.[15] And even when attitudes changed after the executions, attachment to Home Rule still

11 O'Farrell, *The Irish in Australia*, p. 254. 12 Ibid., p. 259. 13 Ibid. 14 *Ballarat Courier*, 29 April 1916. 15 *Melbourne Argus*, 28 April 1916.

held firm in Australia, despite the occasional wobble. A public meeting in Perth, at the end of May 1916, reiterated that a Home Rule Parliament, in accordance with the Act, was essential in the interests of Ireland. As Patrick O'Farrell incisively states:

> the Rebellion was more than a profound embarrassment. It was potentially a dangerous and divisive influence in Australian affairs – which is why many Catholic leaders and Labor politicians wanted to pretend it had not taken place, or was significant, or better still, should be buried immediately under the granting of Home Rule.[16]

Hughes, however, thought otherwise or at least his public utterances would suggest so. Either from pique, guile or ignorance or a combination of all three, he asserted that rabid Irish republicanism was rife in Australia, under the guise of what he termed 'Sinn Féinism'. His pique could be attributed to the November 1916 split in the Australian Labor Party following the rejection of conscription in October. L.F. Crisp has shown that the percentage of Catholics remaining in the Federal Labor Party after Hughes and his supporters had walked out on 14 November, rose from 21% to 45%, and this was seen by Hughes as proof that Irish-Australian Catholics had contributed to his threatened political demise. For most politicians that would have been a daunting prospect but for Hughes it signalled not only oblivion but total oblivion. It is doubtful if there has ever been a politician in Australia who held on to office more tenaciously than Hughes, having fifty-eight years continuous service behind him when he died, aged ninety, in 1952. Therefore the split in 1916 struck a deep chord in Hughes, evoking a corresponding sense of grievance and a desire to search for the perpetrators. One such target was Archbishop Mannix. It is now accepted that Mannix's role in the first conscription campaign was minimal, confined to two public statements,[17] and while Hughes did not make any reference to Mannix during the campaign, he turned on him in its aftermath. First of all he alleged to Lloyd George that Mannix was a 'Sinn Féiner'[18] and, in July 1917, approached the Vatican to have Mannix's freedom of press curtailed, suggesting later that the Australian Government might consider it necessary to avail of the Defence of the Realm Act against Mannix.[19] Finally, in November 1917, Hughes is quoted in the *Sydney Morning Herald* as saying that

16 O'Farrell, *The Irish in Australia*, p. 266. 17 See Fitzhardinge, *W.M. Hughes*, p. 203. 18 Ibid., Hughes to Lloyd George, 17 August 1917. 19 Ibid.

> There is a man . . . who is the real leader of the offending opposition . . . the man whom every German in the country looks to . . . his name is Mannix, and if you follow him you range yourself under the banner of the deadly enemies of Australia.[20]

Such extreme allegations raise questions about Hughes's appreciation of the Irish-Australian mood in 1916–17.

I think it would be correct to conclude that Hughes failed to grasp the depths of Irish-Australian attachment to Home Rule and that he also exaggerated the early significance of the Easter Rising for the Irish Australians. Fitzhardinge correctly maintains that Hughes himself was a Home Ruler though he was unwilling, in my opinion, to share with Ireland the freedoms within the Empire which the 1901 constitution conferred on Australia and which he himself uncompromisingly insisted on at Versailles. Irish Home Rule, for Hughes, was circumscribed. It was limited in the degree of independence it conferred and in its symbolism; it was bereft of any hint of external association but, above all, it entailed total integration within the British Empire. That was the explosive issue as far as Hughes was concerned because, in his calculation, conscription was an integral part of Empire membership and allegiance so that those who opposed it could not be considered Home Rulers in his narrow definition. Accordingly, within these constraints, Hughes could pursue ostensibly contradictory policies of secretly pressing Lloyd George to abandon martial law in Ireland and concede Home Rule while, at the same time, branding all Australian Home Rulers, Sinn Féiners.

The only public overture to Britain between 1916 and 1922 was a resolution passed by both houses of Parliament in March 1917, which expressed the 'hope that a just measure of Home Rule may be granted (without undue delay) to the people of Ireland'.[21] However, in addition, Hughes, either directly to Lloyd George or more often through Keith Murdoch, made confidential approaches along the same lines, though in all instances it is obvious that it was his own, rather than Irish interests, that he had at heart. In these, he pleaded among other things that 'an unsettled Ireland clearly weakened the Empire in the field and in the eyes of neutrals [. . .] the present position in Ireland makes neutrals regard the cry that [Britain] is fighting for the rights of small nations as hypocritical'.[22] In May 1917, he again urged Lloyd George to 'treat Home Rule as

20 *Sydney Morning Herald*, 15 November 1917. **21** Sir Walter Long, Secretary of State for Colonies to R. Munro-Ferguson, Governor General of Australia, 8 March 1917, CO 418/157, Public Record Office, Kew, London (PRO). **22** Hughes to Murdoch, 12 March 1917, copy in F/28/2/1, Lloyd George Papers, House of Lords, PRO.

an imperial question which it most certainly is' and he linked unfounded allegations of the non-enlisting of the Irish in Australia to his political survival.[23] He wrote that 'the non Irish population are going out of Australia to fight [. . .] the Irish remain behind and in any election their voting strength is greatly increased'.[24]

He expressed similar sentiments to Bonar Law where he stated that the Irish question was having a 'very strong disturbing influence on Government policy and its war policy as regards voluntary recruiting'.[25] In a letter through the Premier of New South Wales to his Agent General in September 1916, Hughes maintained that conscription would have a greater chance of being carried 'if the statement could be made [by Britain] that military law [had] definitely ended and Home Rule [was] to be proceeded with'.[26] Hughes also sought to have the Irish question placed on the agenda for an Imperial War Conference scheduled for 1917 but not held until 1918. Again, through Murdoch, he urged Lloyd George

> to accept Asquith's suggestion and say that Home Rule will be remitted to the Imperial Conference on which the British Government, Ulster Nationalists and Dominion Prime Ministers shall sit [. . .] I feel convinced that nothing but good can come out of such a conference. And that the authority of such a conference will supply just that additional weight needed to affect a modus vivendi.[27]

Despite Hughes's threat that he would not be able to attend 'as lack of settlement in Ireland was causing trouble in Australia',[28] Lloyd George refused to accede to his request. In reply, he insisted that the 'Irish question' was a domestic issue of the UK but that if he wished, Hughes could 'discuss Ireland before the conference met' with the British cabinet.[29] Even then, on the substantive issue of Home Rule for all Ireland, it is doubtful if much progress could have been made. In reply to Hughes, Lloyd George intimated that

> It was not possible to settle the Irish question as he pleased. The consent and co-operation of the Irish Parties was essential [. . .] the best help you can render is therefore to induce the Australian Irish to put

23 Ibid., 5 May 1917. 24 Ibid. 25 Hughes to A. Bonar Law, 12 September 1916, Hughes papers, National Library of Australia, Canberra. 26 Premier of New South Wales to Agent General, 19 September 1916, CO 418/148, PRO. 27 Hughes to Murdoch, 12 March 1917, copy in F/28/2/1, Lloyd George papers, House of Lords, PRO. 28 Fitzhardinge, *W.M. Hughes*, p.252. 29 From Lloyd George, through Murdoch, to Hughes, 19 January 1918 (copy enclosed with Murdoch to W.R. Birdwood), W.R. Birdwood papers, Department of Records, British Army Museum.

> pressure on the Irish leaders to accept any settlement which would not involve compelling Ulster by force of arms to accept Home Rule.[30]

Hughes replied, agreeing with Lloyd George that no scheme that 'forces Home Rule upon Ulster' could be acceptable.[31]

However, with the exception of the parliamentary resolution, the Australian public had no inkling of these overtures: the image which Hughes projected publicly was of the abrasive anti-Sinn Féiner, constantly harassed by his disloyal Irish republicans, intent, as he reported to Lloyd George, on 'control of the Commonwealth government'.[32] As the months went by, his allegations became even more absurd and his language more intemperate, creating and fostering that ogre which he sought to dispose of.

In a letter to General Birdwood in October 1916, Hughes asserted that 'the overwhelming majority of the Irish vote had been swung over by the Sinn Féiners. They would vote no in order to strike a blow at Great Britain'.[33] He alleged the following month that the Labor Party machine had been captured by, 'syndicalists of the IWW type plus the Sinn Féiners who foam at the mouth whenever my name is mentioned'.[34] He considered the waterside workers, miners and other unionists' strike in September 1917 as 'an attempt by the Industrialists plus the Sinn Féiners to get even for the defeat on May 5',[35] namely in the general election. He reserved his most extreme and most ludicrous accusations for the Queensland government and for its state police force, both of which he claimed were in the grip of Sinn Féin.

The first incident in Brisbane concerned the distribution of censored anti-conscription information, sneaked into Queensland parliamentary debates by Edward Theodore, the Treasurer, but subsequently confiscated by the Federal Government censor, Captain J.J. Stable. However, during a visit to Brisbane, from a chance remark by Premier Ryan over a cup of tea at his hotel (where they were discussing sugar), that some copies had escaped Stable,[36] Hughes immediately ordered a raid on the government printer. This was carried out, later the same evening, by Stable and his associates. They found the government printing office closed and guarded by armed policemen, who refused to

30 Long to Munro-Ferguson, cable on behalf of Lloyd George, dated 19 January 1917 but dispatched March 1917, CO 418/157, PRO. 31 Hughes to Murdoch, 12 March 1917. 32 Munro-Ferguson to V. Milner, Secretary of State for the Colonies, 15 November 1919, CO 418/178, PRO. 33 Hughes to Birdwood, 20 October 1916, as in H.V. Evatt, Australian labor leader (1940), p. 407. 34 Hughes to Bonar Law, 6 November 1916, A. Bonar Law Papers, 53/4/15, House of Lords, PRO. 35 Hughes to Murdoch, 3 September 1917. 36 For a comprehensive account of these events see Fitzhardinge, *W.M. Hughes*, p. 290.

admit them. Just as Stable was about to climb over the wall, the government printer arrived and let Stable in, saving him the ignominy of sharing Humpty Dumpty's fate or even worse, of being prosecuted for trespass. Hughes himself later turned up at the government printer's office but no incriminating material was found. A complicated series of legal actions followed, which brought the Commonwealth little satisfaction. The second Queensland incident was the well-known affray at Warwick railway station, three days later, where Hughes was scheduled to make a short speech on the way back to Sydney. No sooner had he alighted from the train than two or three eggs were thrown from behind him, one striking his hat and another breaking on a post in front of him. All hell broke lose: Bart and Pat Brosnan, the alleged egg throwers, were set upon by Hughes's minders but not satisfied with that, Hughes, his fists flying, threw himself into the *mêlée,* only to be rescued by Sergeant Kenny in civvies, the senior police officer present, whom Hughes mistook for a civilian, retaliating accordingly. Even after some order had been restored and Hughes began to speak, Pat Brosnan, still at liberty and positioned right in front of the Prime Minister, proceeded to interject while also engaging in finger wagging of an obscene kind. Hughes, beside himself with rage, once again hurled himself into the crowd, screaming at the police to 'arrest the man' and threatening dire consequences if they did not. Hughes was not satisfied with the response and subsequently demanded that Kenny be immediately suspended and prosecuted 'under the laws of the Commonwealth'. Premier Ryan, however, refused to comply and insisted that the Queensland Government would continue to enforce the laws of the Commonwealth and of the State without needing any help from outside. Hughes disagreed and established the Commonwealth police force, sprung not from a revolution but from an egg.

Of greater immediate significance was the interpretation which Hughes put on the two incidents. The Irish names of the main participants, Ryan, Kenny and the two Brosnans, obviously reinforced Hughes's prejudices. In the *Brisbane Courier* of 30 November 1917, Hughes is reported as saying:

> I have been insulted in a cowardly fashion and the police at Warwick apparently acting under instruction from the Ryan Ministry which is utterly opposed to the principle on which Australia and the Empire stand, so far from assisting to preserve order actually connived at the assault upon me and lent their aid to it.[37]

37 *Brisbane Courier*, 30 November 1917.

When T.J. Ryan denied these allegations, Hughes released his reply to the press in which he went even further by claiming that 'the police in your state not only permit but encourage mob rule [. . .] it is a device such as might be expected from one whom Dr Mannix has declared to be an out and out Sinn Féiner'.[38] But he was only revving up! In a telegram destined for George V, Hughes intimated that in Queensland the

> police is honeycombed with Sinn Féiners and IWW and quite apart from the Warwick incident will not only not enforce our laws but openly resists them. This was shown in the case of the government Printers Office where I sent men in plain clothes with a warrant to enter and seize documents and found the place strongly garrisoned by police Sinn Féiners to a man who refused to allow a Commonwealth officer execute warrant [. . .] There are towns in North Queensland where law, state or federal, is openly ignored and IWW and Sinn Féin run the show.[39]

Later Hughes claimed that he had been informed of a plot to seize Brisbane where there were, at the time, only 180 men under arms and 40,000 guns distributed among the general population and that he had sent rifles in piano cases and machine guns in crates marked 'furniture' to prepare for eventualities.[40]

Dramatic stuff! But how accurate? Modern research disputes Hughes's assessment of Sinn Féin penetration into Australian life but, even at the time, Judge Harvey, in his report on Irish Republican internees, drew similar conclusions. In all, there would appear to have been only seven Sinn Féiners – IRA in Australia at the time, of whom none ever served in Ireland and from whom only £20 was ever contributed to the Sinn Féin cause in Ireland.[41] These were drawn from the ranks of the Irish National Association, an Irish republican organisation formed in Sydney in 1915 by Albert Dryer, an Australian with an Irish mother and an Australian-born father of German descent, who never set foot in Ireland but who considered himself Irish through-and-through and wallowed in Celtic sentiment. According to Patrick O'Farrell, by January 1916, the INA had 211 members. In terms of the Irish population this was a tiny number: there were over 22,000 Irish-born people living in Sydney and its suburbs and around 150,000 of Irish descent, not to mention those living elsewhere. At the peak of its membership in 1919, the INA attracted about 1,500 of these. Even this is a gross exaggeration of the support for Irish militancy.

38 *Brisbane Courier*, 5 December 1917. 39 Munro-Ferguson to King George V, 28 January 1918, in Fitzhardinge, *W.M. Hughes*, p. 295. 40 J. Hume Cook, note of conversation with Hughes, 14 January 1929, in Fitzhardinge, *W.M. Hughes*, p. 296. 41 See O'Farrell, *The Irish in Australia*, p. 273.

Dryer had grave misgivings about building the INA through its social programme. The features he wanted did not develop:

> The membership had joined for social reasons often to find suitable matrimonial partners. When eventually a Gaelic teacher was found, few members were interested. The committee affirmed the desirability of establishing a co-operative store to stock Irish goods and manufactures: nothing was done. Nor was anything done about classes in Irish cultural activities – history and the like.[42]

Subsequent events as mentioned, were to indicate that only seven INA members had any revolutionary tendencies and, at most, only fifty plus had IRB sympathies. The Harvey investigation found that they had no connections 'with any enemy person resident in the Commonwealth' and it also confirmed that their contacts with Irish revolutionary movements were infrequent, indirect and tenuous [. . .] and all mediated through America. The most that could be discovered against them was that they had evaded the ban on the entry of Irish-republican newspapers by using Irish seamen.[43] Even when the seven were subsequently imprisoned, there was no outcry from the Irish-Australian community who then, as hitherto, had distanced themselves from such idiosyncratic Irish activities.

It should therefore be apparent that Hughes's response was a gross distortion of the situation. His allegations of widespread Sinn Féin activities were totally fallacious while his ignoring Irish-Australian Home Rule sympathies was inexplicable. The measures which he took against the imaginary Sinn Féiners were equally inappropriate. Under the War Precautions Act, Sinn Féin was proclaimed an enemy organisation in 1918: in 1917 Hughes declared that 'people cannot come to Australia and use it as a vantage ground for the propagation for sedition against the Empire' and accordingly, he insisted on an oath of allegiance to the Empire for all visitors to Australia.[44] Thomas Grattan Esmonde refused and was deported. Only Sir Joseph Cook's intervention, as acting Prime Minister, prevented a similar imposition on Archbishop Mannix on his return to Australia in 1921.[45] Censorship was also tightened. The Customs Act was extended to prohibit literature expressing 'a seditious intention against established government' and a song entitled 'Sinn Féin Volunteers' was prohibited. The film *Ireland a Nation* was censored because it was regarded as

42 Ibid., p. 258. 43 Quotation from ibid., p. 274. 44 *Melbourne Argus*, 29 November 1917. 45 Ibid., 29 July 1921.

an oblique comment on current Irish politics and thus 'likely to cause strife', even though it dealt exclusively with the passing of the Act of Union. The final and most dramatic episode in this sequence was the expulsion of Hugh Mahon MP from the House of Representatives, the only expulsion ever, because of alleged provocative speeches which he made following the death of Terence MacSwiney, Lord Mayor of Cork. Hughes declared in Parliament that 'we will not censure Britain on the ground that one man had died in order to show he believes in Sinn Féin [. . .] and then expects us to laud Sinn Féin whose record of crimes and outrage were not equalled in his lifetime'.[46]

The process of Irish-Australian disenchantment with Home Rule has been well documented, moving from condemnation of the 1916 Rising to tacit approval and then to eventual endorsement at the Irish Race Convention in Melbourne in 1919 which declared in favour of an Irish Republic. It endorsed Ireland's appeal to the nations for international recognition, pledged its support to Ireland's chosen leader Éamon de Valera and suggested that an Australian Irish Relief Fund should be opened to press to a successful conclusion their legitimate claim to complete self-determination.[47] However, there can be little doubt that the progenitors of the metamorphosis owed as much to Hughes's extravagances as they did to events in Ireland. The outcome was a sectarian whirlpool that sucked in a growing number of hitherto unwilling participants and in the process distorted the essentials of the Irish conflict. By that time in Australia the conflict had shed most of its Irish characteristics, ending in an eruption of naked sectarianism, beyond the control of either Hughes or Mannix.

The seeds of this eruption, of course, go way back. Sectarianism has been endemic in Australian society, usually contained but with periodic outbursts as in the 1840s and the late nineteenth century. The 1916 rebellion, and Hughes's distorted response to it, provided even greater scope for the sectarian hedonists. Henry Worrall, Methodist minister in Bendigo, said that 'If he could wake the dead, he would call across the ages, Oh! Cromwell, you are needed more then ever now,'[48] a sentiment endorsed by the Reverend T.B.S. Woodful, president of the Melbourne Federation, when he declared that the only way to deal with Sinn Féiners was to have 'a man of the type of Cromwell at the helm'.[49] But if Cromwell was there he was not alone. The sectarian purveyors did not discriminate, with the *Hobart Mecury* referring in October 1917 to the

46 *Commonwealth of Australia Parliamentary Debates*, November 1920, vol. xciv, p. 6262. 47 Munro-Ferguson to V. Milner, 27 November 1919, CO 418/178 PRO. 48 *Melbourne Argus*, 4 November 1921. 49 Ibid., 9 November 1917.

'Irish Rebellion aided by German gold and led by Catholic priests'.[50] The Reverend T.E. Ruth maintained that 'Russian Bolshevism is an own brother to Irish Sinn Féinism and they are both brothers to German Prussianism [. . .] with a little sister in England, the screaming suffragette',[51] to which Reverend M.D. Forrest MSC retaliated that, to him, 'the soldiers of the Irish Republican Army many of whom I have had the pleasure to meet personally, are the most virtuous and chivalrous young men the world could hope to produce' in contrast with the 'cold blooded murderers, the Black and Tans'.[52] Of these the *Melbourne Argus* had written that 'the advent of the military police brought a ray of light to a vast though silent multitude of loyal subjects who for so long had seen murder and every form of crime stalk the land unpunished',[53] confirming its earlier report in 1916 that 'intense satisfaction is felt in London that government did not accede to the clamour for the reprisal of Connolly and MacDermott',[54] to which Mannix later responded that 'if he could not be loyal to his own people in Ireland he could no longer be responsible to the Empire'.[55] From this the *Hobart Mercury* subsequently deduced that there were 'evil influences operating in our midst [. . .] and it is unhappily only too true that there are centres in which Sinn Féinism is rampant'.[56]

One of the most tangible manifestations of these sectarian outpourings was the refusal of the Victorian government, during the 1919 influenza epidemic, to accept Archbishop Mannix's offer to staff the emergency hospital in the Exhibition Building with nuns.[57] One Protestant parson went so far as to claim that the 'vision of nuns in black habits would lower the recovery chances of non-Catholic patients'.[58] The refusal, according to Mannix, despite the fact that the Exhibition Building had only a quarter of its beds full, 'showed the price the government was prepared to pay to placate sectarians'.[59]

The divisions in society were obviously deep and, at the national level, were reflected in the contrasting motions proposed by Hughes's new national government and those of the remnants of the Labor Party, then in opposition. While the government insisted on the disloyalty of the Irish in Ireland and of their fellow travellers in Australia, in time the Labor Party proved more supportive. At the end of 1917, the Victorian State Labor Party conference supported the right of small nations, including Ireland, to self-determination, which was subsequently endorsed by the Federal Labor Party in May 1918.

50 *Hobart Mercury*, 29 October 1917. 51 O'Farrell, *The Irish in Australia*, p. 272. 52 Ibid., p. 282. 53 *Melbourne Argus*, 1 April 1921. 54 Ibid., 15 May 1916. 55 Ibid., 4 September 1916. 56 *Hobart Mercury*, 13 December 1917. 57 Stanley, Governor of Victoria to Milner, Secretary of State for Colonies, 4 April 1919, CO 418/179, PRO. 58 H. Mac Owen, *Social sketches of Australia, 1880–1975* (1978), p. 61. 59 N. Brennan, *Dr Mannix* (1965), p. 170.

The Australian Trade Union Congress added its weight in June 1921 while, in the following September, the Victorian State Labor Conference carried another motion, this time insisting on a 'hands off Ireland policy' by Britain. Hughes would have wanted an Irish 'hands off Australia' that would have facilitated his Australian imperial designs. He failed, and that failure was due as much to his own responses to Irish-Australian developments as it was to events 12,000 miles away.

3

The Australianization of the Australian Catholic Church: Panico – culprit or victim?

Of all the early Apostolic Delegates to Australia, Archbishop Panico was by far the most controversial and the one that incurred the greatest opprobrium. He was viscerally disliked by the Irish government, by its Ambassador in Australia, T.J. Kiernan and by Joseph P. Walsh, the Irish Ambassador to the Holy See. Kiernan informed F.H. Boland, Secretary of the Department of External Affairs that 'Mons. Panico said to me that no more Irish priests were wanted' in Australia.[1] Kiernan also accused Panico of great rapaciousness maintaining that

> He established a scale of charges for his attendance at functions, from £250 for the consecration of a bishop down to £20 for receiving debutantes at Catholic balls, and that when he visited convents, nuns locked away the best ware of the house as he was in the habit of giving orders to transfer silver etc. to his motor car.[2]

Joseph P. Walsh was even more scathing. In a conversation with Monsignor Montini, the future Pope Paul VI, in February 1947, Walsh asserted that Panico 'was a disaster for the Church, was a worldly prelate and had made the whole idea of Italian representation of the Holy See in foreign countries unpopular'.[3] He [Walsh] was also amazed at the docility of the Irish-born Australian bishops towards Panico, concluding that he had 'a strong feeling that the Australian air makes our people a little bit funky *vis-à-vis* Rome'. 'Imagine the reactions', he wrote, 'of our own bishops at home to an individual of the Panico type. They could and would freeze him out in six months.'[4] Even Mr de Valera, the Irish Taoiseach, without ever having met Panico considered him 'a man whose anti-Irish prejudices are known and who has treated distinguished Irish prelates in Australia so badly'.[5]

1 Kiernan to Boland, 20 May 1947, MS. D12 I, National Archives of Ireland, Dublin (hereafter NAI). 2 Kiernan to Department of Foreign Affairs, Dublin, 11 October 1947, MS. D12 I, NAI. 3 Walsh to Secretary of Dept. of Foreign Affairs, 11 February 1947 MS. D12, NAI. 4 Walsh to Boland, 14 June 1947, MS. D12, NAI. 5 Boland to Walsh, 3 April 1947, MS. D12, NAI.

However, by far the most pungent of all Panico's critics was, surprisingly, the Australian-born Minister of Immigration, Arthur Calwell. Whether from his long-standing friendship with Irish-born prelates in Australia or from his own genuine appreciation of the work done by Irish-born priests, he unleashed a tirade of accusations against Panico both verbally when in Rome, and in correspondence with Monsignor Montini, the Vatican Secretary of State, that bordered on the defamatory. Firstly he singled out aspects of Panico's behaviour in Australia which he found outrageous: for example, Panico's preference for favourable treatment for 'wealthy internees' such as 'Prince del Drago' and for what he described as 'other known Fascists like the Alcorso brothers', all this to the neglect of ordinary Italians. Calwell, in fact concluded that 'Panico often represented not the interests of the Holy Father but the interests of the Italian state,'[6] and that:

> his continued interference in secular matters that are of no concern to any Delegate and are the source of such resentment, has worried and annoyed those Cabinet Ministers acquainted with his doings so that the ordinary good layman cannot believe [that these actions] would be sanctioned by Christ's Vicar if he were aware of the circumstances.[7]

Calwell next referred to Panico's actions 'without consulting anybody in recommending a Coadjutor (who was not wanted) for Melbourne' and likewise in proposing that 'Cairns should be taken from the Augustinian Fathers and made a Bishopric without provision for its future' and finally in transferring the 'headquarters of the Propagation of the Faith [...] from Melbourne to Sydney'. He also accused Panico of waging a 'long and bitter vendetta against Archbishop Mannix, who had done such single service for the Church in Australia'. Accordingly, Calwell while not asking for the removal of Panico requested that 'Rome take heed'.[8]

The response of the Irish-born bishops in Australia was more circumspect. They accepted that Panico was entitled to appoint Australian clerics to bishoprics but they argued that the timing of these was premature, that the scale was excessive and they deplored the fact that in bypassing Irish-born priests for clerical advancement, these were being disenfranchised. They reserved their more strident criticisms for appointments to higher ecclesiastical offices such as archbishoprics and ultimately the cardinalate. They deplored the

6 Calwell to Vicar General of the Society of Jesus, 2 September 1947 MS. D12, NAI. 7 Calwell to Secretary of State to His Holiness, 23 October 1946, MS. D12, NAI. 8 Ibid.

transfer of the Australian Archbishop Gilroy to Sydney on the departure of Archbishop Sheehan as they had banked on that premier see being retained by an Irishman and next they were outraged by the elevation of Archbishop Gilroy to the cardinalate over the head of their own candidate, Archbishop Mannix. They held Panico responsible for these moves. Archbishop Duhig of Brisbane, an Irishman, refused to attend the reception for Cardinal Gilroy on his return from the 'Red Hat' ceremony in Rome in 1946 and, according to Duhig's biographer, T.B. Boland, 'was formally correct rather than welcoming' when the new cardinal visited Brisbane.[9] It was that same prelate who raised these issues with the Pope on one of his rare *ad limina* visits to Rome in 1947. Duhig referred to the matter of 'the exclusion of the Irish-born priests from the Australian Episcopate' and he informed the Pope that it was deplored by the Irish in Australia as well as by the Irish in Ireland who regard it as a cruel blow, a reflection on their race and ingratitude for their sacrifices and their fidelity to their faith, and particularly to the Holy See. He concluded by pointing out that 'this exclusion was reacting adversely on the Church in Australia' because 'it has not only been unwarranted, but too sudden' and he recommended that 'such changes should come gradually' as 'otherwise they not only fill the young native clergy with pride' but also 'with an idea of self-sufficiency which was not justified'.[10]

Whether that was justified or not, Panico's actions undoubtedly endeared him to the Australian-born priests, especially those in the Manley Union. These obviously were elated at having their own priests appointed bishops, the ultimate accolade being when Gilroy was created cardinal in 1946. While few in number, Panico could also draw on support from among Irish-born clerics, the most notable being Patrick O'Donnell, ironically, the future coadjutor to Duhig and his eventual successor. But Panico's most valuable ally was, unquestionably, his friend Cardinal Agagianian, Cardinal Prefect of Propaganda Fide, under whose jurisdiction Australia still fell. Agagianian promoted Panico's cause at Rome, defended him in the face of the criticism already referred to and even provided accommodation and hospitality whenever Panico visited Rome. Panico was indeed a contentious personality; he had bitter enemies and loyal friends. He could not be ignored and his period in Australia was a most divisive one. But were these divisions there on his arrival and if so, could they have festered even without Panico or, on the other hand, were they of Panico's making, stemming from his deficiencies and from his reactions to

9 T.P. Boland, *James Duhig* (1986). 10 Dr Duhig's, 'Audience with the Holy Father', September 1947, MS. D12, NAI.

developments in Australia? If it was the former, then Panico could be seen as a mere siphon. However if the latter, then he was a catalyst.

Divisions in the Australian Catholic Church were deep-rooted. The more recent ones dated from the end of the nineteenth century following concerted efforts to train native priests in Australia which led to a clash between the products of these Australian seminaries and with those who had arrived from Irish ones. Until the Prefecture of Cardinal Fumasoni Biondi, the Australian-born clergy lacked mentors in high places. But with the appointment of a series of Apostolic Delegates by Fumasoni Biondi to Australia, their interests were not only recognised but were consciously promoted. Thus even before Panico arrived, the combat lines had been drawn, the agendas were in place and the determination of all parties to pursue their own interests, well established.

Firstly, the de Valera government and its representative in Australia, T.J. Kiernan, sought to foster and advance the Irish dimension of Australian society and looked to the Irish Catholic clergy for support. These could draw on the experience of the second half of the nineteenth century, when the Gaelicisation of the Catholic Church in Australia contributed substantially to the Hibernicization of large sections of Australian society, thereby transplanting 'old Ireland' to the new world. In the Irish version of pluralism disparate cultures were the raw material of, and the catalyst for, Irish proselytism, with the activities of the Catholic clergy in Australia paralleling the role being played in post-revolutionary Ireland by the so-called 'Irish Irelanders'.[11] But they misread the situation, especially Kiernan, to such an extent that the latter had to be cautioned by Mr F.H. Boland against restricting his 'activities too much to Irish and Catholic circles in Australia'. Kiernan also failed to recognise that by 1947, only 45,000 out of a population of approximately 6.8 million people were born in Ireland compared with 177,000 out of a population of 400,000 ninety years earlier,[12] and that following the Irish Civil War, Irish-Australian interest in Irish affairs sharply declined mainly because of disgust with events in Ireland. De Valera's reception on his visit to Australia in 1948 was decidedly tepid.

Similarly with the distribution of Catholic priests in Australia; following the foundation of the seminaries of Manley in Sydney and Corpus Christi in Melbourne, the proportion of Australian-born and trained priests in Australia exceeded that of Irish-born by the 1930s. Despite the fact that the vast majority of these Australian-born priests had Irish antecedents, by the 1930s, these

11 Boland to Kiernan, 27 February 1947, D12 I, NAI. 12 Wray Vamplew (ed.), *Australian historical statistics* (1987), p. 8.

tended to distance themselves from their Irish roots and to strike an Australian note, much to the chagrin of Irish diplomats. Joseph Walsh, the Irish Minister Plenipotentiary in Rome, attributed that to 'British propaganda and to a gross ignorance about our country'. According to Walsh, 'they are still swallowing stories of the 'pigs and caubeens' type, so the temptation of snobbery and Britishism found them an easy prey'.[13] Earlier, however, he did concede that 'for what it was worth, Australia was not getting the better type of Irish priests'. Once again he confided in Boland that

> I am informed that the Maynooth missions and their new foreign Mission Societies in Ireland are taking the cream of our young men and that All Hallows and Thurles get the leavings. It has also been said that thirty years ago the great majority of them would have been sent home long before they finished their courses.[14]

Whatever the merits of these observations, there can be little doubt that there existed a chasm between the Australian-born and the Irish-born priests in Australia and that the former viewed the latter with some degree of disdain. Dining with the Australian-born Bishop Young in 1951 Kiernan observed that in the course of conversation, Young had said that 'the Irish priests in Australia were not as well read as the Australian trained priests. They do not read books.' Bishop Young also noted that 'It is a pity that correct speaking is not taught in Irish seminaries. Many of the young priests coming here from Ireland speak almost unintelligibly'. And Kiernan concluded that 'underneath the skin, both Bishop Young and Archbishop Beovich are hostile to Irish priests'.[15] Walsh deplored these divisions between what he termed 'the two sections of our people' because in his view when 'we are not united they can serve British or Italian ends according to the Vatican or Italian needs of the moment.' 'They must be helped' he wrote 'in responding to the aspirations of the Holy Ghost'.[16] Thus, well before Panico's arrival in Australia there were deep divisions within the Catholic ecclesiastical community and, generally speaking, the balance seemed to be swinging in favour of the local-born clergy.

That would appear to have been in line with long established Vatican policy. With the exception of the first Papal Delegate to Australia, Archbishop Cerretti, all observers, even the most hostile to Panico, concede that the Australianization of the Australian Catholic Church was stated policy of Propa-

13 Walsh to Boland, 9 October 1948 MS. D12, NAI. 14 Walsh to Boland, 17 June 1947, MS. NAI. 15 Kiernan to Secretary, Department of External Affairs, 17 September 1951, Dl2 I, NAI. 16 Walsh to Boland, 17 June 1947 MS. D12, NAI.

ganda Fide and was implemented by Monsignors Cattaneo and Bernardini, Panico's immediate predecessors.[17] Kiernan even alleged that Cardinal Fumasoni Biondi had given directions to all these delegates to 'down the Irish'.[18] Archbishop Duhig subsequently informed Kiernan that 'on Mons. Bernardini's arrival in Australia as Papal delegate in 1933, he is said to have declared that he would put an end to Irish influence in the Church here'. It was also alleged that Monsignor Cattaneo 'wished to be attended only by Australian priests'[19] at religious ceremonies. And finally Cardinals Tardini, Ottaviani and Montini confirmed for Joseph Walsh that 'the policy' of the Holy See in Australia was 'that of Australianizing the Church there as far as possible' and that 'it was part of a general policy all over the world'. These also noted that 'the French priests in China were resisting, even priests in the English-speaking countries were doing so, but the policy had to go ahead. It was the result of very long and very mature deliberation and was considered to be in the best interests of the Church'.[20]

By the time of Panico's arrival in Australia in 1935 more than half the priests were Australian-born, and, as Boland has shown 'Sees across the continent were tumbling to the Australians – Townsville and Geralton in 1930, Lismore and Wilcannia – Forbes in 1931, Rockhampton in 1932 and Port Augusta in 1934', prompting an acquaintance of Archbishop Duhig to observe that 'appointments of Australians to Bishoprics are becoming a bit monotonous'.[21] It is also apparent that Irish-born bishops resented these appointments and did all they could to frustrate them. In the case of the appointment of an archbishop to Perth in 1932, Duhig, again, according to Boland, 'made it clear to the delegate that he could pursue the Australian policy only at the cost of a break with the Irish. The appointment of anyone but Redmond Prendiville (Irish born) would be a *casus belli*'.[22] And in a subsequent letter to Mannix, Duhig wrote that 'if we are not vigilant anything might happen'[23] by which he meant that Australians would be appointed to Australian archbishoprics. These, however, were also to go. With the untimely resignation of the Irish-born Bishop Sheehan (Archbishop Kelly's coadjutor in Sydney) in 1937, that Archbishopric was also vulnerable to an Australian appointment. There was little the Irish-born bishops could do to halt the flow of events. They could only hope to delay them and trust that, by stag-

17 See Calwell to Montini, Secretary of State to His Holiness, 23 October 1946, MS. D12, NAI. 18 Kiernan to Boland, 20 May 1947 MS. D12, NAI. 19 Duhig to Kiernan, 20 May 1947 MS. D12, NAI. 20 Walsh to Boland, 2 July 1947, MS. D12, NAI. 21 T.P. Boland, *James Duhig*, p. 287. 22 Ibid. 23 Ibid., p. 289.

gering Australian appointments, they could still retain their eminence within the Australian hierarchy until their own eventual demise. They did not reckon, however, on the remarkable longevity of Irish-born prelates in Australia.

It is therefore clear when faced with the attitude of the Irish-born bishops in Australia and bound by his own instructions from Propaganda Fide, Panico found himself in an explosive situation on his arrival in Australia in 1935. In a letter to the Prefect of the Congregation of Propaganda Fide, dated 5 October 1937, (and cited only by B.A. Santamaria though without indicating its location), Panico reviewed that situation. He alleged that the nature of both his predecessors' recall had been 'engineered in a form which immensely discredited the apostolic delegation'. He then accused the bishops (mainly Irish) of overriding the wishes of the priests in the appointment of bishops because while 'the clergy would formally go through the procedure of an election [...] the bishops of the province would pay regard to the result only when it returned the person they wished to see elected' and this he attributed to the 'undue intervention of certain bishops'. He next alleged that 'the custom had grown up whereby almost every bishop could choose for himself not merely an auxiliary bishop but a coadjutor with the right of succession in the future'. Thus, as Monsignor Cattaneo so accurately expressed it, 'Episcopal seats were mortgaged beforehand.' Panico then drew on one of his own experiences in the case of the nomination of a coadjutor for Hobart:

> Even though Mons. Simonds was unanimously elected, even though he was regarded by all as a most worthy and learned person, how much was done by the Archbishops of Adelaide and Brisbane to exclude Mons. Simonds and to secure the appointment of an Irish intriguer who did not even receive one vote from the Tasmanian clergy.

He accused the Irish bishops of using 'devices' that 'have not always been the cleanest' in securing these appointments and he singled out Archbishop Mannix as the 'deus ex machina' of these operations. According to Panico, Mannix had perfected the art of bypassing the Apostolic Delegate, the best example of which was the appointment of Sheehan to Sydney unknown to Monsignor Cattaneo.[24]

Panico, however, was determined to rectify that situation and to follow his instructions to the letter even if that meant antagonising a large and influential section of the Australian hierarchy. By so doing he also hoped to enhance

24 B.A. Santamaria, *Daniel Mannix* (1984), pp. 182–4.

his credentials back in Rome. The tragedy for Panico and for the Catholic Church in Australia was that in pursuing these objectives he continuously overstepped his brief essentially because of his many personal shortcomings. He was venal, he was avaricious, he indulged in unwarranted jibes and actions, he identified with only one section of the Australian priestly community and, in his personal dealings he was aloof and authoritarian. As such, he ironically provided hostages to fortune for the Irish-born privileged, if embattled, prelates because he allowed them focus on his own defects rather than on their lack of generosity and accommodation.

He did not inform Mannix that he was about to provide him with a coadjutor with the right of succession. Mannix was seventy-eight at that time and should have considered passing on the mantle to a younger man but he did not. He was still in good health despite the occasional fainting fit and was determined to hold on to his diocese for as long as he could. Still, at his age, there was nothing sinister in appointing a coadjutor. It was the manner in which the appointment was made and not the appointment itself that reflected badly on Panico. As we do not have Panico's side of the story, because of Vatican archival policy, the only possible excuse for his behaviour was his belief that had Mannix had forewarning of an imminent appointment, he would have objected to it or even tried to frustrate it. As it was, the first Mannix heard of the appointment was when, according to Kiernan, the 'Coadjutor presented himself' at Raheen,[25] though Santamaria does mention that Mannix did 'receive notice by telegram shortly before'.[26] Simonds himself, (the man who had been unsuccessful in Hobart), the unfortunate coadjutor, was as surprised as Mannix with his elevation. Kiernan also maintained that 'when Mons. Panico goes to Melbourne, he never sees the Archbishop' and that there was 'a complete rift between him and Archbishop Mannix'.[27] However the Irish bishops' biggest grudge against Panico was their belief that he deprived their idol, Mannix, of a Red Hat. To quote Santamaria's eloquent account:

> While it was in one sense natural that if a Cardinal's Red Hat was to be conferred on an Australian it should be conferred on the Archbishop of Sydney; and while it is conceivable that the Vatican could believe that in distant and unimportant Australia to confer the Red Hat on Mannix would arouse the hostility of the Anglo-Saxon establishment, the suspi-

25 Kiernan to Boland, 26 October 1946, MS. D12, NAI. **26** B.A. Santamaria, *Daniel Mannix*, p. 186. **27** Kiernan to Boland, 26 October 1946, MS. D12, NAI.

> cion must remain that insofar as Panico was involved in the nomination, his feelings against Mannix would play a part. No one close to Mannix at the time witnessed the slightest sign of envy or disappointment – perhaps because he was master of himself, perhaps because he did not experience either feeling.[28]

That view was generally held at the time. In a letter to Boland, the year after the appointment, Walsh reported that 'it is being said that the Holy See knows that Panico deliberately misinformed them about Mannix and accordingly made them give the Hat to the wrong man'.[29] Panico subsequently denied that allegation. Eleven years later in conversation with Leo McCauley, the then Irish Ambassador to the Vatican, Panico said that 'he had nothing to do with it [. . .] If I could appoint Cardinals, I would appoint myself Cardinal.'[30] Until the Vatican Archives are opened, one can only speculate. Panico did not deny his involvement in the nomination when in Australia nor did he ever conceal his antipathy towards Mannix. It was also consistent with his Australianization policy to have proposed an Australian for the Red Hat and who other than Gilroy, the bishop whom he himself had transferred from Port Augusta to Sydney early on in his ministry in Australia. His subsequent denial was in absolute terms and so did not cover his undoubted involvement, as delegate, in the process. Ultimately, the only issue was his motive in denying Mannix the position and he did little to allay suspicions that his opposition was vindictive.

Finally there appears to be little dispute about Panico's demeanour and manner: following his appointment as Nuncio in Peru in October 1948, Kiernan wrote of a lunch which he had with 'a fair cross section of the Sydney clergy, regular and secular' at which 'they spoke freely of the general sense of relief at what is regarded as Archbishop Panico's removal' because as Kiernan observed 'his manner towards the priests was dominating and abrupt and towards the Irish priests rude, as he disliked them merely for being Irish. [...] He had an indiscreet and sharp tongue, and uncharitable; and is an outstanding example of the reverse of the sign by which the early Christians were known, 'How these Christians – love one another'.[31]

In conclusion, Panico did implement Vatican policy but in such a way that he allowed opponents to these changes to hide behind criticism of his own personality defects. Thus Irish diplomats and Irish-born prelates in Australia,

28 B.A. Santamaria, *Daniel Mannix*, p. 188. 29 Walsh to Boland, 14 June 1947, D12, NAI. 30 McCauley to Secretary of Department of External Affairs, 31 May 1958, MS. D12, NAI. 31 Kiernan to Boland, 11 October 1948, MS. D12 I, NAI.

by directing their criticism at Panico, could conceal their fundamental opposition to any immediate alteration in the status quo. These had also been critical of Cattaneo and Bernardini, but were forced to temper their objections because these delegates' demeanour and/or urbanity did not provide a cover for Irish vested intransigence. In that sense, the abrasive and venal Panico was a godsend! They could oppose him on personal grounds without having to confront basic policy changes or reveal their own stubbornly held objectives. They neither recognised nor acknowledged the spiritual successes of worldly prelates in the long history of the Catholic Church. That would not have suited their case. Their shock and outrage at another Italian being appointed to succeed Panico, Monsignor Morella,[32] did shed some light on their true motives but fortunately for them, Morella informed Kiernan 'that he would counsel Irish Australian Catholics to keep to the Irish traditions'[33] with the result that Kiernan could inform Dublin that 'Mons. Morella has done much to undo the damage caused to the Church in Australia by his predecessor.'[34] Morella had put the clock back and the Irish retrieved some of their lost ground to such an extent that by 1951 the Irish Ambassador to Australia informed Frank Aiken, the Irish Minister for External Affairs, that the 'friendly Delegate Morella, was worried at the shrinkage of Irish priests coming to the Australian mission' and that the Holy See had realised that 'the line taken by Apostolic Delegates has had to be reversed and that the Catholic Church still has to depend and will long continue to depend on Ireland for servants in the mission field'.[35] Defeats in the past could now be attributed to Panico and the Holy See was exonerated. Duhig already had informed the Pope that the Irish people 'cannot believe that Your Holiness would tolerate any reflection on their character much less any injustice against them'.[36] These criticisms were reserved for Panico.

32 Walsh to Boland, 7 December 1948, MS. D12, NAI. 33 Kiernan to Boland, 10 March 1949 MS. D12, NAI. 34 Kiernan to Department of External Affairs, 5 October 1951, D12, NAI. 35 Irish Ambassador to Australia to Aiken, 22 October 1951, MS. D12, NAI. 36 Duhig to Holy Father, September 1947, MS. D12, NAI.

4

The British government and Archbishop Daniel Mannix

Much has been written about Archbishop Mannix's overseas trip in 1920; the magnificent send-off which he received in Melbourne, even missing the train to Sydney because of the crowds; his triumphant tour across the United States, addressing large gatherings, sharing platforms with President de Valera, and promoting the Sinn Féin cause with obvious relish; the British government's refusal to allow him land in Ireland and his subsequent 'arrest' by the British navy off the coast of Ireland; and finally his landing in Penzance and his seven-month tour of those British cities not proscribed by the authorities.[1] However, the question still remains as to why a trip by an expatriate archbishop, ostensibly to visit his aged mother in Charleville, should have assumed such international significance.

The answer to these questions is to be found firstly in the personality of the archbishop whose national and international stature had risen enormously in the seven years since he arrived in Melbourne. His career in Ireland, while distinguished, had generally been uncontroversial. He was very much of a man of his time and of his class. Like the sons of many large tenant farmers in the late nineteenth century he proceeded to study for the priesthood at Maynooth after completing his secondary studies at his local diocesan college, in his case, St Colman's, Fermoy. His political objectives, if he had any, were those of the Irish Parliamentary Party whose pursuit of Home Rule and a more secure stake in their properties by tenant-farmers coincided with the moderate aspirations of most of Mannix's class. There would be no social revolution, merely a change in the location of government with minor alterations in its composition. It was not embarrassing for Mannix to entertain royalty at Maynooth as many of his apologists alleged; on the contrary, most of his class would have been quite honoured to have done so at the time. His handling of the 'O'Hickey Affair' was also quite consistent – what was not, in Mannix's opinion, was

1 See for example: Frank Murphy, *Daniel Mannix, archbishop of Melbourne* (1948); Niall Brennan, *Dr Mannix* (1965); Walter A. Ebsworth, *Archbishop Mannix* (1977); Colm Kiernan, *Daniel Mannix and Ireland* (1984); B.A. Santamaria, *Daniel Mannix* (1984).

the lack of support from his own establishment, both clerical and lay, and it was that factor more than anything else which caused him to revolt in later years against the values of his former peers. The fact that the 'O'Hickey Affair' lost him an episcopal appointment in Ireland, in particular Dublin, was to colour his subsequent relations with his homeland. He went as an exile to Australia not only in space and distance but also as an exile from his own class and from the establishment that he had so assiduously cultivated in the past.[2] He would not make the same mistake again.

In Australia he found ample opportunities for his lately-discovered radicalism which in a strange way allowed him create his own establishment, with himself at the epicentre in juxtaposition to the prevailing social, clerical and political hierarchies in that country. His radicalism was less that of a reformer and more that of an advocate of traditional Celtic aspirations and Roman Catholic orthodoxy in an alien environment. The opposition which that engendered set Mannix in an heroic role and provided him with a wider forum than the administration of a local diocese would otherwise have afforded. His support for the 1916 rebellion in Ireland, his anti-conscription stand in the two conscription referenda in Australia and his espousal of state aid for Catholic schools were to produce tailor-made issues that ensured the maximum amount of controversy. As a result Mannix was already a national celebrity in Australia when he decided in 1920 to pay his *ad limina* visit to Rome. That trip was to thrust him onto the international stage.

It was the timing and the route taken as much as the local standing of Archbishop Mannix which transformed that trip from a routine meeting between the Pope and one of his bishops into an international incident. Had Mannix taken a different route, especially had he omitted the United States, and gone direct to Ireland and then to Rome, it is doubtful if he would have evoked so violent a response from the British government. It was the tone of his speeches in the United States and his rapturous reception there that was viewed with alarm by the British and caused the British government to take such a strong line on Mannix's landing in Ireland. In his address to the Catholic Summer School at Plattsburg, New York, on 14 July 1920, Dr Mannix stated that:

> Ireland is ruled by an alien government. I see no other way out but American recognition of Mr de Valera. Some have said England is a friendly nation. No, England never was a friend to the United States.

2 Frank Murphy, *Daniel Mannix*, p. 9, where a contemporary is quoted as saying that Mannix 'mixed a good deal in general society in Dublin, and in particular in medical society. He was a member of the Papal Household Club in London, and as president met and entertained all manner of men.'

> When your fathers fought, it was against England. Ireland has the same grievance against the same enemy, only ten times greater. I hope Ireland will make a fight equally successful. England was your enemy; she is your enemy today; she will be your enemy for all time. England is one of the greatest hypocrites in the world. She pretended to be your friend in the war. Now that the war is over, she tells you to mind your own business.[3]

The British Consul-General in New York, Mr G. Armstrong, closely monitored Mannix's movements and speeches in the United States and kept the Foreign Office informed of these. Quoting from the *Daily News* of 20 July 1920, Armstrong informed London that 14,000 had attended Mannix's meeting in Madison Square Gardens where Mannix had said that he was 'going to Ireland to kneel at the graves of the Easter rebels murdered by brutal British bullets'. Mannix apparently also expressed regret that 'Ireland's invader had not been German'. 'I can speak for the British Empire' (laughter) he said 'that if you (United States) went to war with England, the Empire would not'. Also present at that meeting was Archbishop Hayes of New York whose first mention of Britain was greeted by hisses which, the *Daily News* reporter observed, 'he smilingly encouraged'.

Had Mannix travelled either in the previous year or in the following year or even earlier in 1920, it is most likely that he would have been allowed land in Ireland. However, because of the deterioration in the Irish security situation, especially in July and August 1920, it was considered inadvisable to allow Dr Mannix access to that country. Both General Sir Nevil Macready, Commander of Forces in Ireland and Major-General H. Tudor, responsible for the police, reported to London in July and August 1920 on the deterioration. Tudor 'feared that the RIC could not last much longer as they did not consider that they were being properly supported'. He alleged that there was a feeling of insecurity among the police because of (1) the release of the hunger-strikers and (2) the fact that not a single criminal had been brought to justice for murder.[4] Macready repeated these observations in a memo on Ireland which he prepared for W.S. Churchill, Secretary of State for War, written on 26 July 1920 but not forwarded until 6 August, in which he considered it 'necessary that increased power should be given to those for maintaining the government of the country if the RIC is to be saved and a semblance of law and order preserved'.[5] These reports were most unwelcome for the Cabinet as they

3 *The Times*, 16 April 1920. 4 CAB 24/109, C.P. 1693, 23 July 1920. 5 CAB 24/110, C.P. 1750,

were also faced with the growing concern both in Ireland and in Britain, as well as internationally, about the deteriorating health of Terence McSwiney, Lord Mayor of Cork, who was then many months on hunger strike. The British government was most anxious for calm in Ireland and some semblance of normality, as it was also trying to steer the Government of Ireland Bill through Cabinet, which involved balancing the demands of Unionists with those of the Nationalists while promoting Britain's own interests. Dr Mannix's visit could not have come at a more inauspicious time.

In fact, had he even arrived in June of that year, he may well have been allowed land. On that occasion the Cabinet decided that 'in view of the serious effect which they were informed would be produced on public opinion in Ireland by prohibiting the Archbishop from landing in Ireland, it could not sanction this procedure'.[6] Instead, fearful that Dr Mannix might also be appointed Archbishop of Dublin, the Secretary of State for Foreign Affairs was instructed to make clear to the Vatican its displeasure with Mannix's behaviour and to indicate 'the undesirability in the present state of Irish affairs of appointing as Archbishop of Dublin a person of pronounced and publicly proclaimed anti-British sentiment', and also 'the desirability of finding some employment for Archbishop Mannix outside the United Kingdom'. Count de Salis, the British representative at the Vatican, was indeed happy with the outcome of his representations. He was assured that there was never any intention of Dr Mannix being appointed to Dublin and that the rumour of appointment had not 'even the appearance of probability'. He was also informed that 'the Holy See will support His Majesty's government in prohibiting a landing in Ireland but would not forbid it if the British authorities allowed it',[7] a position which either de Salis misinterpreted or which was perhaps later reversed by the Vatican because a month later de Salis was obliged to report that 'it is hard not to suspect desire in certain quarters of the Vatican to take back or minimise the condemnation of Archbishop Mannix'.[8] Thus even as late as June 1920, Dr Mannix could have got off with a rebuke from the Vatican but would still have been allowed enter Ireland, in spite of his anti-British statements in Australia and his pronouncements in the United States. It was the security situation in Ireland which caused the British government to adopt a harder line on the Mannix visit. Unfortunately for Dr Mannix, his visit to Ireland coincided with a comprehensive review of the Irish political and security situation which took place in London on 23 July 1920 when the decision to ban him from landing was

6 August 1920. 6 CAB 23, No. 21, meeting 24 June 1920. 7 de Salis to Foreign Office, 28 July 1920. 8 de Salis to Foreign Office, 25 August 1920.

taken, not by the Cabinet as such but rather by this wider body which included military and police personnel and their Unionist sympathizers.[9]

However, the Defence representatives and the Ulster Unionists did not have all their own way at that meeting. They were strongly challenged by the joint Under-Secretaries for Ireland, Sir John Anderson and Mr G. MacMahon, who were supported by F.W. Wylie, the law adviser. These argued that repression alone would not solve the Irish problem. Sir John Anderson felt that 'General Tudor was too extreme' and that 'when the time came to take off Martial Law there would be no material left with which to work for a solution to the Irish problem'. Mr Wylie feared that General Tudor's approach 'would create an atmosphere of intense hostility and resentment' because 'the Irish would regard it as another piece of English tyranny' as a result of which 'more and more of the loyalists would tend to go over to the rebels'. . . . 'Already', he said, 'there was a complaint by loyalists against the stoppage of race trains'!! He also urged that the Six Counties should be left under British rule and not be given a separate parliament. But the moderates failed to carry the day. Had they succeeded, it is most unlikely that Archbishop Mannix would have been banned.

Instead it was the recommendations of General Tudor that were accepted. Amongst these were included the institution 'of a special penalty of flogging imposed for the cutting of girls' hair and outrages against women' and also he recommended that 'no tribunal should function except as a court martial' and that 'court martial be the tribunal for all crimes'. He also advised that identity cards be introduced 'as have been done by the army of occupation in Germany' and that 'passports should be necessary for entry into Ireland'. He further recommended that 'Cardinal [a red hat conferred by Tudor!] Mannix should not be allowed to land in Ireland' which was apparently agreed to without dissent. However, the fact that the Irish situation committee, a hawkish body, chaired by Walter H. Long, First Lord of the Admiralty, at its meeting six days later advised the Cabinet that a 'person serving in the Irish government should not in any circumstances be permitted to hold communication with Sinn Fein except on the basis of the government's expressed policy, namely, the repression of crime and the determination to carry through the Government of Ireland Bill on its present mainlines',[10] suggests that the moderate civil servants had indeed posed a threat to the designs of the Unionist-influenced military and civilian personnel involved with Irish affairs. So that

9 CAB 24/109 C.P. 1693, 23 July 1920. **10** CAB 24/110, C.P. 1703, 29 July 1920.

even on the occasion when the decision to ban Dr Mannix was taken, there was still the slight possibility that it might not be carried.

Having once decided to ban him the British government did not waver. A Cabinet meeting on 2 August 1920 reaffirmed the 23 July decision and elaborated further on the implications of the ban. It was decided on that occasion that 'should Archbishop Mannix succeed in landing in Ireland, the Irish executive should take any step necessary to arrest and deport him' and that 'the Law Officers of the crown should examine the speeches of Archbishop Mannix and ascertain whether they contain anything of a nature which would admit his prosecution in this country or by the Australian government'.[11] By August, the British Government were intent on even arresting him in Britain, certainly a change from their response the previous June. And even as late as November 1920 the British Government refused a request of William Adamson, chairman of the Labour Party, 'to have the matter reconsidered and see if it is not possible to allow him pay the visit he much desires'. Even though Adamson had stressed that 'Mannix had not approached the party in any way' and that previous publicity 'which was given to the matter had died down' and that Mannix 'does not appear to be a dangerous person', the Cabinet was not moved.[12] The influence of Walter Long was again evident. Though not directly involved, he wrote to the Cabinet, disputing Adamson's assertions and highlighting once more Dr Mannix's remarks in the United States. As a result five years were to pass before Archbishop Mannix was in a position to visit Ireland. By then his mother had died.

In these ways, a seemingly innocuous visit by a prelate to his mother was transformed into an international incident that has become part of Irish-Australian folklore. It might have been otherwise, as I have argued, though it is doubtful if any other course would have appealed to the Archbishop himself. Anything else would have been out of character with the 'post-O'Hickey' Mannix.

11 CAB 23, No. 22, 2 August 1920. 12 CAB 24/114, C.P. 2091.

5

The Empire at work: Australia, Britain and Ireland at the Ottawa Conference

The Ottawa Conference came close to collapsing on 15 August 1932, despite the many months of preparation by all sides and the intense negotiations which had taken place since its opening on 21 July. The main reason for the impasse was differences over duties on British meat imports: the British did not want them, all the other countries did. Much has been written about the Ottawa Conference, but remarkably no one has satisfactorily explained how the crisis was resolved or even mentioned the bizarre role played by the Irish in the proceedings. Kottman attributes the rescue to Prime Minister Ramsay MacDonald;[1] Middlemas and Barnes to Baldwin,[2] while Drummond is not sure.[3] Ramsay MacDonald did not intervene while Baldwin may or may not have met Stanley M. Bruce. He would have had little time for such a meeting because of commitments with the British delegation, and there is no mention of it taking place in the records. In any case, Bruce did not require any prompting from Baldwin to change his mind. His concern for the Empire was sufficient. However, in all these accounts the part played by J.H. Thomas is underestimated while Ireland's involvement is ignored. Hopefully, the present article, by analysing the momentum which develops when national interests are being promoted in an imperial context, may shed some light on this crucial moment during the Ottawa Conference.

Prior to 1930, there was little official communication between Australia and Ireland despite the large numbers of Irish in the Australian population. What little contact took place was indirect, mainly through the British government and often that was hostile as in the case of W.M. Hughes during World War One. Even those of Irish descent such as J.H. Scullin and J. Curtin, tended to distance themselves from Ireland, once in power. This of course could not be said of British-Irish or for that matter British-Australian relations. In the case of the former, official dealings were out of all proportion to the size of the pop-

1 R. Kottman, *Reciprocity and the North Atlantic triangle, 1932–38* (1968) p. 31. 2 K. Middlemas and J. Barnes, *Baldwin* (1967), p. 682. 3 I.M. Drummond, *Imperial economic policy, 1917–39* (1974), pp. 259–63.

ulation involved while with the establishment of a High Commission in London, Australia ensured that she would not be ignored at Whitehall. But there was another forum that purported to transcend bi-lateral exchanges, namely the British Commonwealth, laterally, the British Empire. But that evoked contrasting responses – the Irish believed that the Commonwealth was still the British Empire, the Australians wished it was, while the British knew it was not. This undoubtedly limited its scope though on those intermittent occasions when the member countries gathered for Conferences, still called Imperial until 1937, a momentum was generated that was often independent of the individual participants. One such occasion was the Imperial Economic Conference held in Ottawa from 21 July to 20 August 1932.

The Irish attended, but only just. Since the foundation of the Irish Free State, Irish governments had an ambivalent attitude toward these conferences, seeing in them one other vestige of British imperialistic domination but now that they were partially independent they would not let that upset them.[4] Until 1930 they attended all conferences, refusing however to accept British government hospitality lest they be compromised. In 1930, they relented on that act of national self-denial, much to the delight of E.J. Harding, a Dominion Office official, who saw it as 'good augury'[5] though when the list of the Irish delegation was submitted, numbering seventeen plus secretaries and typists, George V was appalled and asked what 'will the British tax-payers say',[6] ignoring the fact that the Maharajah of Bikaner alone brought his son, his Comptroller of Household, his private secretary, his surgeon, two aide de camps, an Indian male stenographer and four Indian servants. The Irish at least only had their wives and these attended infrequently. The King still blamed Balfour who had reaffirmed the principle of hospitality in 1926 but he consoled himself with the thought that 'the Irish Free State will reciprocate by a gesture of increased friendliness!'[7] That however, was more problematic with the advent to power of Eamon de Valera in 1932 and for a while the Dominion Office was apprehensive about the Irish attendance at Ottawa. Being a recognised abstentionist, having abstained from the Treaty negotiations in 1921 and from the Dáil until 1928, de Valera could have been expect-

4 Writing to Sir Harry Batterbee at the Dominions Office in 1930, William Peters, the British Trade Commissioner in Dublin, observed that 'The position is that on the political side the tendency is to disassociate the IFS from the UK in international politics whereas on the purely economic side, disassociation is not precisely welcome'. 24 Sept. 1930, DO 35, 90/4011/2601, Public Record Office, London (hereafter PRO). 5 E.J. Harding to J.H. Thomas, 27 July 1930, DO 35 118/1/F4265, PRO. 6 Clive Wigram to J.H. Thomas, 11 August 1930, DO 35 118/1/F4265, PRO. 7 Clive Wigram to J.H. Thomas, 16 August 1930, DO 35 118/1/F4285, PRO.

ed to abstain from the Imperial Economic Conference and until April 1932 that seemed most likely. But following British retaliation to his withholding of the annuities, de Valera reluctantly concluded that something might be salvaged at Ottawa.

Strange to say, that reluctance to participate in an Imperial Economic Conference was shared by Britain herself, who until 1930 at least, had sought to steer Imperial Conferences away from economic issues and focus them instead on constitutional, defence and cultural matters, using them as a means of maintaining the tenuous links which bound Commonwealth countries to the motherland. The Empire as such was a useful device for promoting British interests but it had its limitations especially when Dominions competed with the mother country as was increasingly the case with agriculture. The simplest expedient for the British was to keep such issues off the agenda but when that was no longer possible, she resorted to such bribes as the Empire Marketing Board, damned, even before its foundation, by E.J. Harding as a 'convenient waste-paper basket for schemes of no particular interest'[8] and also the Imperial Economic Committee which was in fact precluded from dealing with questions involving tariff policy as it was obliged to obtain the consent of each interested Empire government before commencing any economic survey. Even as late as 1930, Britain gave little indication that she was prepared to alter her attitude towards Empire economic issues. British cultivation of the Empire was therefore selective; the choice owed more to her own needs than it did to her imperial responsibilities though the latter sentiment could also be invoked to camouflage sectional interests. Being a free trade country until 1932 and exporting more to and importing more from foreign countries than it did from the Empire, Britain did not tolerate Empire interference in her domestic economic affairs. However, following the 1929 crash and subsequent Depression, Britain found that she could no longer rely as formerly, on foreign markets for her overseas trade and as a result was forced for the first time to turn to the Empire and to take it into her economic confidence.

With Australia it was otherwise. Unlike the Irish, Australians never had direct representation at Westminster and even when retired prime ministers like Sir George Reid found their way to the House of Commons, these represented British, not Australian interests. But also unlike the Irish, Australians had long since pressed for a greater say at Westminster and again unlike the Irish, that had not been conceded to them. It was indeed ironic that a country like Australia which had willingly divested much of its autonomy to Britain,

8 E.J. Harding to Llewellyn Smith, 17 July 1932, CO352/262, PRO.

especially in the sphere of foreign policy, even postponing the implementation of the Statute of Westminster for over ten years, should have obtained so little representation at Westminster or enjoyed so few confidences. Denied access to centre stage, Australia sought to have the spotlight focussed on the wings and saw in Imperial Conferences ready made devices for that purpose. Australians were accordingly keen participants at Imperial Conferences. The more far-ranging the agenda the better; the more frequent the meetings the ideal, preferably even in continuous session. 'Imperial sentiment' according to Leo Amery in 1925 was 'strong in Australia, though a passion, almost religion in New Zealand'. But that oozing enthusiasm was seldom matched by results. The Australian input into major imperial developments was indeed slight. Deakin has deplored that fact as early as 1887, observing at the Colonial Conference in that year 'the powerlessness of great, populous, wealthy and important communities to gain a hearing with a foreign power or even in the Imperial Parliament'.[9] That was still the case in 1930: Australia had been by-passed when Balfour made his declaration in 1926 and the Statute of Westminster implementing that decision, found scant support in Australia. Now that Britain had changed heart and opened up an Imperial Conference to economic issues, Australia recognised that, at last, she could play a role nearly equal to the mother country – it would now be possible to observe the British Empire at work with no more dedicated workers than the Australians. Australia hoped according to Hankinson, the British representative in Australia in 1932, that 'Ottawa would result in a multi-lateral agreement providing for similar preferences and conditions of entry into the United Kingdom for goods from all parts of the Empire'.[10]

But while Australia might have liked an Empire solution to the prevailing Depression, nationalistic demands soon emerged with each of the three sides pressing for a remedy for their own particular problems. The Irish had been hard hit by Britain's retaliation to Ireland's failure to pay the annuities and so, unlike other participants who were looking to Britain for outlets for their agricultural surpluses, Ireland, perhaps unrealistically sought outlets for hers in Commonwealth countries. Also, shielded by the anonymity of imperial discussions, Ireland hoped that it might be possible to hold furtive meetings with the British on the annuity question. Haunted by the legacy of its wayward borrowing for ill-advised wheat expansion in the 1920s, Australia had now to find the foreign currency to meet these interest and capital repayments, and

9 Quoted in A.G.L. Shaw, *The story of Australia* (1960), p. 183. **10** W.C. Hankinson to Undersecretary, Dominions Office, 8 March 1932, DO 35 240/8813H/13, PRO.

that was made more difficult by the Depression. As most of these borrowings had been in Britain, interest and capital repayments in 1930 alone involved a transfer of over 24 million in gold bullion or 50% of total Australian exports to Britain.[11] This drain on Australian reserves could not be sustained indefinitely and Australia came to the conclusion that the only remedy was increased exports to Britain, the income from which would help service and eventually liquidate the debt though surprisingly the chief British trade negotiator in Australia at the time, Robert Dalton, saw no future for Australia's principal exports of wool and wheat in the British market and would have preferred to have seen 'the discussions follow the line of financial assistance to Australia such as guaranteeing certain funds and conversions on the one hand and trade benefits to Great Britain on the other'.[12] Australia did recognize the problems posed for its wool and wheat in the glutted British market but instead of pursuing monetary solutions, she pinned all her hopes on greater access to the British market for other agricultural commodities. This was to have near-disastrous consequences for Australia and came close at a later stage to wrecking the Commonwealth itself.

The British delegation arrived at Ottawa totally confused. As already mentioned, there was no precedent for an Imperial Conference devoted exclusively to economic matters, and the British like precedents. Further, the severity of the Depression took her by surprise in spite of the fact that economic decline for most of the 1920s in Britain meant that unlike other Western capitalist countries, there was not much further for Britain to fall by 1929. Protectionist policies in her former world markets forced Britain to turn to the Commonwealth for economic relief and that was indeed a novelty. The national government was split on what should be done, with the National Labourites opposed to higher food prices while the major partner, the Conservatives condoned these if they led to better opportunities for British industrial products abroad. Thus like many of the foundation professors of economics at Australian universities who were trained only in philosophy, the British delegation hoped to work up their briefs on the boat out but unlike the academics, they did not get far. According to Geoffrey Whiskard, a Dominion Office official with the British delegation, 'we had all the materials [. . .] for formulating a policy, but made very little use of them' and he recommended that 'if such an occasion ever occurs again, that Britain should have something faintly resembling a policy before she starts'.[13] He was right. Even after three weeks in Ottawa, the

11 CAB 32/101 – 107233, Table III, PRO. 12 Dalton to SOS Dominion Office, 23 Jan. 1932, DO 35 240/8831H/10, PRO. 13 Whiskard to Harding, 22 August 1932, DO 35/121/61, PRO.

United Kingdom delegation in a moment of self-attrition conceded that 'before discussions with the Australians could take place it was necessary that the United Kingdom delegates should make up their minds exactly what their policy was'[14] and the Prime Minister, Ramsay MacDonald, back in London was understandably confused and equally unhelpful. In a telephone conversation with J.H. Thomas, MacDonald said that he found the entire subject 'very complicated' but that he hoped 'that some solution' would be reached that 'could be unanimously accepted'.[15] And so the three delegations arrived in Ottawa with the Australians in search of meat outlets, the Irish in search of allies, and the British in search of a policy.

However, whatever their original designs for the Conference, most delegates soon discovered that Ottawa developed a momentum of its own with new issues being introduced and earlier positions being blurred. While the Conference retained its essential imperial character, the interaction of delegates and the general atmosphere led eventually to a degree of fragmentation. As expected, the opening statements made the appropriate references to the Empire and to the inter-dependence of all its members. But within a short time Bruce had suggested 'that the United Kingdom delegates should [. . .] see each delegation separately'.[16] By the end of the conference negotiations were being carried out on a two to two or even one to one basis with Chamberlain and Hailsham conferring nearly hourly with Bruce and Gullett while the leader of the British delegation, Stanley Baldwin, like Brer Rabbit, mostly 'lay low and said nuffin'. Private discussions also took place, often the result of the many social events laid on by the Canadians. For those delegates not fully employed at formal sessions, and there were many of these, especially from the large British delegation of seven Cabinet Ministers and as many more officials and advisers, these exchanges were not only valuable but also helped to relieve their boredom.

It would, of course, have suited my purposes splendidly had I uncovered close fraternising between the Irish and the Australian delegates, but alas there is no such evidence. It is highly unlikely that the aloof and imperious Bruce and his equally remote colleague Gullett, would have found much empathy with the garrulous bonhomie of O'Kelly or the apparently furtive shuffling of Lemass. Also the Australian pair were heavily burdened with formal negotiations. That was not the case with J.H. Thomas, the British Secretary of State for Dominion Affairs, who according to Whiskard 'was quite interested, but

14 Minutes of Meeting of UK Delegation, 10 August 1932, CAB 32/101, PRO. 15 Ibid., 16 August 1932, CAB 32/101, PRO. 16 Ibid., 2 August 1932, CAB 32/101, PRO.

regrettably carried no weight with his colleagues' so that he was 'more in evidence on social rather than committee occasions'.[17]

This may well have suited him. Thomas had always done most of his work by discussion. He seldom read papers in the office and virtually never wrote a minute, except perhaps to his bookmaker. He relied heavily on bluff and was frequently crude. According to Joe Garner, an official in the Dominion Office, Thomas greatly offended Prime Minister Lyons during the Silver Jubilee celebrations in 1935 when he greeted him with the jest that 'Moss Brothers must be making a fortune out of him' because Thomas had seen him at various functions in frock coat, evening dress and court uniform. But while Thomas may have been ignored by many of his colleagues at Ottawa, they could not ignore the fact that he was the confidant of his National Labour colleague, the Prime Minister, and so in the last resort it was Thomas who provided the crucial link between Downing Street and Ottawa. Meanwhile, however, he was mostly left to his own devices which mainly entailed fraternising with O'Kelly and Lemass with whom he was apparently temperamentally in tune. On one occasion when Whiskard went to see Thomas, he found him playing bridge with two of the South African advisers and with Lemass. Whiskard reported the rumour that Thomas hoped by the end of the Conference to have won enough to settle the annuities question though 'whether, if so, he would turn it over to the Exchequer was another question'.[18]

Professor Drummond has stated that 'there were no Anglo-Irish discussions'[19] at Ottawa and in one sense he is right – they merely played cards! However, he is incorrect in alleging that because there were no formal talks, that negotiations did not take place. On the contrary, some of the most highly sensitive negotiations of the entire Conference took place in that informal context and in a way that could have had far-reaching implications for the entire Commonwealth, not least for Australia.

Predictably, the well-known long-distance negotiator, Eamon de Valera, did not attend and only issued one positive instruction to his negotiating team at Ottawa, namely that before any agreement was reached, that he be notified of the content and that 'the delegates shall await an intimation from the President that the Executive Council agrees before entering such an agreement'.[20] The remaining instructions were negative. The delegates could not enter into any commitment that might conflict with the government's policy of self-

17 Whiskard to Harding, 5 August 1932, DO35 121/61, PRO. 18 Whiskard to Harding, 25 July 1932, DO35 121/61, PRO. 19 Drummond, *Imperial Economic Policy*, p. 248. 20 Cabinet Minute 6/45 No. (III) 8 July 1932, State Paper Office, Dublin Castle (hereafter SPO).

sufficiency so that it was unlikely that a reduction of Irish tariffs would be bartered for markets elsewhere.[21] Nor could they entertain an agreement which 'would leave the Free State at the mercy of combines of Great Britain and elsewhere'. This was indeed remarkable in view of the dramatic deterioration in the Irish balance of trade from a deficit of 11 million in 1930 to 16 million for the twelve months to 30 April 1932, the bulk of which was due to Great Britain. This was recognised by O'Kelly in his opening speech in which he referred to the 'special difficulties' that had recently arisen 'which affected about 85% of our trade and which may involve substantial changes in the form and direction of that trade as well as in the internal economic structure of our country'.[22]

The Irish achievements at Ottawa were accordingly slight. Canada agreed to allow Irish goods into Canada on the same terms as those from Great Britain and Northern Ireland in exchange for an Irish undertaking not to discriminate against Canadian goods in Ireland[23] and the South Africans also conceded preferences to Irish hosiery, tractors and stout in exchange for Irish preferences on their fruits and wines.[24] While no agreement was made with Australia at Ottawa because according to Gullett, 'Mr Bruce and myself have had our hands so full with general United Kingdom considerations', Australia did extend the 'preferences which the Commonwealth grants to the United Kingdom' but only until such time as a new Treaty 'with the United Kingdom came into force'[25] which was a few weeks later. With so little to show, the Irish delegation must surely have resented the limitations imposed by their instructions and also perhaps have regretted that de Valera himself had not attended. Being present and perhaps caught up in the mood of the Conference, he might have been more flexible though it is doubtful if he would have enjoyed the same camaraderie as O'Kelly and Lemass did with J.H. Thomas.

Thomas himself was not constrained by instructions, in fact, Britain's problem was the absence of any instructions, but in a strange way Thomas had become the victim of his current appointment. Not noted hitherto for his imperial sentiments, his office as Dominion Secretary created its own expectations, and Thomas did not disappoint. Eventually he became convinced that even as late as 1932 the Empire still mattered and this distortion was reinforced by the heady atmosphere at Ottawa. His relationship with O'Kelly and Lemass

21 Ibid., No. 11, SPO. 22 Report of Imperial Conference held at Ottawa, 1932 presented to both Houses of the Oireachtas by Minister of External Affairs (Dublin, 1932), p. 86, SPO. 23 Agreement between IFS and Dominion of Canada, 20 August 1932. 24 Trade Agreement between Union of South Africa and IFS, 20 August 1932. 25 H. Gullett to S. Lemass, 22 August 1932, file S6157A, SPO.

further deluded him into believing that a solution could be found to the Irish problem within an imperial context, thereby elevating British-Irish negotiations to a plane that had not been originally envisaged. Thomas sought to prove that the Empire still worked.

He was ably abetted in that design by his Permanent Head in London, Sir Edward Harding, the source of most, if not all, of Thomas's ideas. Harding was at least, by profession, a great Imperialist and in Thomas's close association with the Irish delegation, Harding saw a golden opportunity for a grand Imperial gesture, that was not sullied by the unseemly haggling over vulgar economic preferences. As a result he believed that the Empire would be enhanced, that British-Irish relations would be regularised and most important of all that the fledgling Dominion Office would get most of the credit.

The solution proposed by Harding and readily accepted by Thomas was that:

> at the last meeting of heads of delegations when we are finally settling the proposals, which will be formally confirmed at the closing plenary session, Bennett speaking for Canada and supported by Bruce and Havinga, speaking for Australia and South Africa would nominate their Chief Justice or some other judge of the Supreme Court to examine into the validity of the financial agreement existing between us, which are the cause of the present dispute and to make a report thereon to those governments, which your government could accept or not. It being understood that pending the receipt of their recommendations there should be an economic truce between the two governments, that is, that we should revert to the status quo that existed before tariff legislation passed by both sides.[26]

This approach had all the advantages, according to Harding in his overtures to a reluctant Prime Minister, of a solution to the 'dispute being found within the British Commonwealth' and that if accepted, 'Mr de Valera would have gone far towards committing himself to the position that the future of the Irish Free State is within the British Commonwealth' and that finally the British would be

> able to enter into the World Economic Conference and the negotiations for debt settlement with the United States unhampered by the existence of an economic war between ourselves and the Irish Free State

26 File S6157A, SPO.

> and on the contrary, helped by the fact that an Imperial Conference has provided an approach to the solution of our difficulties with the Irish Free State.[27]

For this scheme to work it was essential that the Ottawa Conference succeed, that the Commonwealth heads of delegations cooperate and finally that de Valera participate. All three requirements were most doubtful. The Conference was getting more and more bogged down in meat negotiations, the Commonwealth leaders had not been advised of the plan and on past experience, de Valera was hardly likely to respond to a Commonwealth initiative.

J.H. Thomas however, was determined to succeed even if that entailed sacrificing traditional labour policies. Solving the Irish problem and strengthening the Empire apparently meant more to him than local British political considerations. As a result, what mattered most at Ottawa was not the months of preparation in London and in Canberra, nor was it the negotiating skills of Bruce and Gullett nor was it the initial ineptness of the British delegates but rather it was Thomas's championing of Ireland's cause, ironically unknown to the Irish themselves. On its own, that gesture might appear insignificant, but by a remarkable coincidence, Thomas's intervention coincided with the imminent breakdown of the Australian meat negotiations and so with the possible collapse of the Conference itself. Prompted by Irish considerations, Thomas proferred a life line that had it been availed of, would have conceded all the Australian demands and would have ensured that the Commonwealth survived to break the British-Irish impasse.

From their very first meeting with the British delegation, the Australian negotiators at Ottawa had emphasised the importance for them of greater access to the British market for their meat and at higher prices. With monotonous regularity they tended to conclude each round of discussions liturgically with a cry for meat! but they got nowhere. While the British were genuinely confused throughout and oscillated in their private discussions from one possible response to another, when eventually they made their minds up very late in the proceedings they refused Australia's request for import duties on foreign supplies of meat into Britain, thereby precipitating the major crisis of the Conference.

Even though meat accounted for only about 10 per cent of Australian exports, slightly more than half the value of Australian wheat exports and

27 Appreciation by E.J. Harding of Proposals for Arbitration read by him over the telephone to the Prime Minister, Ramsay MacDonald, 17 August 1932, DO 35 397/111/ 390, PRO.

only double that of apples,[28] the Lyons government considered that 'meat production formed a considerable portion of the income of a large number of our primary producers' and so he 'authorised the delegation at Ottawa to place this subject in the forefront'.[29] However in view of the fact that meat exports were also a very small part of total meat production, this concentration on meat to the detriment of all else would appear to have been exaggerated. Further, frozen meat exports from Australia were no substitute for chilled Argentinian meat and Australian scientists failed to make much progress before 1932 in adapting Australian meat exports for distant markets.[30] No chilled beef was exported in 1931, only £1,000 worth in 1932 and £5,000 in 1933.[31] Australian demands could thus only be based on future potential, not on current output.

Britain's decision of 15 August that no 'duty should be imposed on imports of foreign meat into the United Kingdom'[32] would appear to have been final – the logical outcome of the National Labour Party's insistence that no duties be imposed on meat, even excluding it from the February Import Duty Act, despite a willingness by Chamberlain and Hailsham to entertain such a proposition. This is Professor Drummond's view and he quotes at length from a memorandum by Thomas in which Thomas states 'that the limits of all possible concessions were long past [. . .] he [Thomas] could not assent to the proposal that the decision of the previous day not to impose tax upon meat, should be reversed'.[33] It is also true that by the middle of August, the British delegation was becoming more and more embittered by the antics of the Canadians and of the Australians. Whiskard wrote to Harding that Neville Chamberlain had said that 'he had put up at Ottawa with insults from Bennett and Bruce such as he would never have imagined it possible that he should have done',[34] while Thomas informed Ramsay McDonald that by 15 August 'the United Kingdom delegates had now reached the stage where they were being held up to blackmail and ransom'[35] leaving a sour note that persisted for long after the Conference itself. In September 1932 Sir Henry Fountain of the Board of Trade advised Whiskard in the matter of pig meat 'not to give way too readily to the Australians to continue screwing concessions out of us till the last possi-

28 Statement showing the values of the principal commodities imported into the United Kingdom from Australia since 1931, Appendix II, DO 35/749/01/45, PRO. 29 Ottawa Conference – *What it means to Australian farmers* in CP103/12 Bundle 20, p.17, Australian Archives (hereafter AA). 30 J.M. Bastian et al., *50 years of food research* (1979), pp. 2–24. I am grateful to Dr K.T.H. Farrer, OBE, FTS for this reference. 31 DO 35 749/01/45, PRO. 32 Meeting of UK Delegation, 15 August 1932, CAB 32/101, PRO. 33 Drummond, *Imperial economic policy*, p. 260, quoting from Premier, 1/112: 'The Australian and New Zealand negotiations and a duty on meat', expanding O(UK)(32) 54th Conclusion, Minute 4, for the Prime Minister. 34 Whiskard to Harding, 19 August 1932, DO 35 121/61, PRO. 35 Premier, 1/112, 'The Australian and New Zealand negotiations'.

ble moment'.[36] But Thomas's decision of 15 August was however, reversible. In fact, it was his dramatic 'Damascus-like' about turn on 16 August, that came close to rescuing the Conference from possible total collapse.

It was the vehemence of Bruce's response to the British decision on meat which fortuitously coincided with the climax of Thomas's own private negotiations with the Irish delegates, that prompted him to re-consider his emphatic rejection of Australian demands the previous day. Bruce had replied that

> so far as they were concerned, the conference was at an end and it would be necessary to start again de nouveau, and examine inter alia the question of the maintenance of Australian preferences to the United Kingdom and of the United Kingdom preferences to Australia.[37]

This was no bluff and was recognized as such by Thomas. On hearing of Britain's decision to impose quantitative restrictions rather than import duties on meat, J.A. Lyons immediately cabled Bruce and instructed him 'on no account make any further substantial concessions without consulting us' and in a second cable that same day, Lyons stated that he could not 'agree to any treaty which does not contain safeguards against cuts in Australian meat exports to Britain'.[38] Thus with the Conference in tatters, Thomas could no longer make a great imperial gesture towards solving the Irish problem and it was that latter factor more than anything else which caused him reluctantly to withdraw his objections to import duties on meat. The Irish were now playing a crucial role unknown to themselves at an Imperial Conference.

At an early morning meeting of the United Kingdom delegation on 16 August, Thomas informed them

> that after the meeting of the previous evening [. . .] he had considered the matter to which reference had not been made, mainly, the effect of the failure of the Conference on the position in the Irish Free State. The more he thought about this particular factor, the more imperative it seemed to him was the need for making the Conference a success. He had therefore resolved to tell the Prime Minister that the point had now been reached where success or failure appeared to depend on tariffs on meat and in the circumstances he [Thomas] would risk the imposition of that tax rather than that the Conference should fail.[39]

36 Fountain to Whiskard, 20 Sept. 1932, DO 35 273/9261/7, PRO. 37 Meeting of UK Delegation, 15 August 1932, CAB 32/101, PRO. 38 Lyons to Bruce, 19 August 1932, CP/103/12 Bundle 21, AA. 39 Meeting of UK Delegation, Tuesday morning 16 August 1932, CAB 32/101, PRO.

In his telegram to the Prime Minister, Thomas said that 'in making this recommendation myself to you, I am subordinating all my personal feelings, although I feel desperate'.[40] While MacDonald believed that the concession on meat 'would mean the resignation of possibly five of the Cabinet Ministers at home' in a later telephone conversation that day with Thomas 'he said that he had been unable to communicate with other Cabinet Ministers in the United Kingdom . . . and that he hoped that the United Kingdom delegates would do their best to arrive at a solution which would be unanimously accepted.'[41] However he did not censure Thomas or veto his proposition.

In the event, J.H. Thomas did not have to compromise his National Labour principles nor did Ramsay MacDonald have to risk a split in his Cabinet because at the last moment Bruce gave way while de Valera held tight. Both reactions were indeed predictable. As Prime Minister in the 1920s, Bruce had not propounded the Balfour Declaration nor as a member of the Lyons Cabinet had he pressed for the adoption of the Statute of Westminster in Canberra – he was an Empire man and was even prepared to deviate from his Prime Minister's instructions in order to ensure that the Empire survived. While Baldwin may have influenced Bruce's decision as Middlemas and Barnes suggest,[42] it is doubtful if he needed such prompting. De Valera had never indicated that he would accept Commonwealth arbitration – on the contrary, he had always opposed it. On 15 July 1932 when in London for discussions with MacDonald, he had stated 'that he was not willing to accept arbitration by any form of tribunal drawn from within the British Commonwealth'.[43] Even while the Ottawa Conference was in session, Miss Ellis, a friend of Mrs de Valera and a sister of Lady Parmoor, brought a proposal from Dublin, endorsed by de Valera, in which there was no mention of Commonwealth intervention. He would only agree to a 'Conference of equal numbers of delegates appointed by each government to be held as soon as possible in Dublin' and only if the British government would withdraw the Irish Free State Special Duties Order with the sum in dispute 'to be paid into the Bank of International Settlement'[44] until a solution had been found.

The participants had reverted to form; Britain did not have to make an economic concession to a Commonwealth country; Australia had to give way on meat while Ireland distanced itself from the Commonwealth and the entire imperial process. In their closing addresses Britain engaged in the usual impe-

40 Telegram Thomas to MacDonald, 16 August 1932, CAB 32/101, PRO. 41 Meeting of UK Delegation, 3 p.m. 16 August 1932, CAB 32/101, PRO. 42 Middlemas and Barnes, *Baldwin*, p. 683. 43 CP 291/21, SPO. 44 Ibid.

rial platitudes, Australia did the same but with greater conviction while Ireland merely thanked Canada. O'Kelly spoke of the charm of Bennett, apparently only recognised by the Irish delegation and concluded with a 'parting prayer that God may prosper this capital city and the Canadian nation'.[45] There was no mention of Britain or of the Commonwealth.

Had Australia held firm for another twenty-four hours and obtained her duty on meat, she would surely have been unwittingly indebted to the Irish for providing the circumstances that led to that concession. Accounts of the Ottawa proceedings are thus incomplete without reference to the strange way in which Irish and Australian interests impinged on one another and became entwined in an imperial wrangle.

45 Report of Imperial Conference, p.154.

6

Conditional loyalties: Australia, Ireland and the decline of the Dominion Office

The Dominion Office differed from other government departments because its loyalties were never as clear cut; while other departments of state could profess direct allegiance to the government of the day, the Dominion Office had no such immediate focus. As well as being 'responsible for handling relations between the government in Britain and each of the governments of the Commonwealth overseas', Malcolm McDonald, one of its most distinguished Secretaries of State observed that it also acted as the 'official Secretariat organising Commonwealth Conferences and attempting to co-ordinate the views of all these governments on important international matters of Commonwealth concern'.[1] Accordingly, it was answerable not only to its political masters in London, but also to the rest of the Commonwealth, including Ireland. As such, there was a possible conflict of interests that was only avoided by the astute balancing by Dominion Office officials of the Dominions' respective aspirations, though these were invariably weighted in Britain's favour. The skills needed for that task drew heavily on the accumulated wisdom of a tightly-knit department. But these skills were sharpened by Dominion Office officials' appreciation that without a Commonwealth they themselves had no raison d'être. Devotion to duty and departmental expertise owed as much to self-preservation as it did to the department's split loyalties.

Departmental cohesion was reinforced by the opposition it experienced elsewhere in Whitehall. The Foreign Office resented ('despised', according to Deirdre McMahon)[2] the Dominion Office's involvement in diplomatic affairs. Traditionally an elite service, the Foreign Office had attracted public school products and members of the aristocracy; the Dominion Office remained a part of the home civil service with a less socially elevated intake. Now it was the latter that was filling the prestigious diplomatic posts, such as High Commissionerships, in the Dominions. Friction was also apparent in some of the Dominion Office's relations with the Board of Trade. The latter, in its deal-

1 J. Garner, *The Commonwealth Office* (1978), p. xii. 2 Deirdre McMahon, *Republicans and imperialists: Anglo-Irish relations in the 1930s* (1984), p. 34.

ings with Commonwealth countries was invariably only concerned with Britain's own trading needs, whereas the Dominion Office also had the interests of the Dominions at heart and so was willing to concede a share of the British agricultural market to them, often against the wishes of the British Department of Agriculture and of the Board of Trade. The Treasury had from the very beginning opposed the establishment of a separate department catering for the Dominions, preferring instead to retain responsibility within the Colonial Office. In fact it was because of Treasury opposition, especially that of Sir Warren Fisher, that the establishment of a Dominion Office was delayed for more than twenty five years after the Dominions themselves had been established. The Treasury's objections were based essentially on finance because it considered that a separate department was merely duplicating existing duties and so adding to costs. Even more demanding were the views of the Lord Chancellor, Lord Sankey, in 1932, in a letter to the Prime Minister, where he maintained that 'the Dominion Office does not contain the best brains in the civil service',[3] while Deirdre McMahon also alleges 'other ministers and officials didn't rate its efficiency very highly either'.[4]

Regrettably for the Dominion Office it could not obtain political relief for these disabilities because of the low ranking of the department in the Cabinet and also because of the calibre of some of its Secretaries of State. Most politicians were not attracted to it. When the National Government was formed in 1931, Eden relates that he hoped for a post in the Foreign Office, but Baldwin warned him that Ramsay MacDonald wanted his son to go there. Eden made it clear to Baldwin that he himself preferred the Foreign Office – 'of course you would, of course you would', replied Baldwin.[5] In appointing Inskip to the Dominion Office in 1939, Chamberlain remarked in unambiguous terms 'it is not a very absorbing department. You will be available for Committees.'[6] In fact in the crucial last months before the war, Chamberlain worked with a very small inner group which did not include the Dominion's Secretary. When in 1938 the Offices of the Dominion Office and the Colonial Office were put in charge of a single Secretary of State (Malcolm MacDonald), the *Daily Express* rejoiced at the 'excellent decision' and continued 'the Dominion Office is no more than a post office. Its functions could be merged with those of Major Tyron's (the Postmaster General). Indeed that is perhaps the best place for it. The Dominion's Secretaryship will add to Mr MacDonald's dignity, but it will

3 Ramsay MacDonald papers, 30/69/701, Sankey to MacDonald, 15 August 1932, Public Record Office, London. 4 McMahon, *Republicans and imperialists*, p. 34. 5 A. Eden, *Facing the dictators* (1962), p. 19. 6 T. Inskip, *Diary* (1939) p. 230.

add nothing to his responsibilities.'[7] That was also the view of Dominion Office officials themselves. Geoffrey Whiskard, one such official, observed at Ottawa in 1932, that 'J.H. [Thomas] is not very strong stuff to lean on [. . .] he is quite interested but carries no weight with his colleagues'.[8]

It is therefore not surprising that initially staffing in the Dominion Office should have been miniscule, but what is indeed remarkable is that in 1928, for example, an establishment of thirty one of whom a mere thirteen were administrative officers should have had to cater for a Commonwealth of six Dominions, namely Australia, Canada, New Zealand, South Africa, Newfoundland and the Irish Free State. It is even more remarkable that with such wide-ranging responsibilities and with such limited personnel, that, according to Joe Garner, himself a Dominion Office official, senior officers did not arrive in the office before 11.00 a.m., though he also mentioned that they would 'stay late and not leave before 7.00 p.m. as a rule'.[9]

Faced with these handicaps, it is surprising that the Department was able to function at all; but it was that very fact which concentrated officials' minds on where they could be most effective and so justify their continued existence as a separate department. They soon discovered that they were most successful when mounting salvage operations to limit the harm caused by differences between the Dominions and the British government or, for that matter, between the Dominions and other government departments. Dominion Office officials' close ties with their civil service counterparts in the Dominions and the skill with which they managed or even manipulated their own Secretaries of State were essential in that respect. Only on rare occasions, however, did the Dominion Office take the initiative itself and then, even more rarely, did it succeed. That suited the Irish better than the Australians. Because the former were in almost constant conflict with the entire establishment at Whitehall, the Dominion Office had plenty of opportunities for rescue operations and usually it was successful. The Australians, on the other hand, expected more from the Dominion Office, believing that it complemented the work of their own High Commissioner in London. That was too much to ask; the Dominion Office, because of its mandate and its constraints, could not become an extension of the Australian High Commission in Britain. The problem, however, for Australia, was that it failed to recognise that fact, and so persisted with its exaggerated and unrealistic expectations of that department.

7 *Daily Express*, 28 October 1938. 8 G. Whiskard to E.J. Harding (Permanent Under Secretary, Dominion Office), 5 August 1932, DO121/61, PRO. 9 Garner, *The Commonwealth Office*, p. 32.

Dominion Office officials maintained excellent relations with both Irish and Australian civil servants, especially with J.P. Walsh, Head of the Irish Department of External Affairs and with the Irish representative in Britain, J.W. Dulanty, and likewise with S.M. Bruce, Australian High Commissioner in Britain, and with his economic advisor, F.L. McDougall. These contacts were particularly valuable when relations at ministerial level were icebound. The contacts between Irish and British officials were most fruitful in the strained atmosphere of the 1930s. With de Valera at his most perplexing, feigning total disregard for Britain at home – the visionary looking inwards across the bog of Allen as far even as the Atlantic to the United States – while privately hinting, albeit obliquely, at possible accommodation, politicians and officials in Britain were, understandably, bewildered. Mr Walsh, for example, visited London with Mr de Valera's knowledge, but not necessarily with his approval. Lord Granard considered Mr de Valera to be a 'borderline between genius and insanity. I have met men of many countries and have been governor of a lunatic asylum, but I have never met anybody like the President before. I hope that the Almighty does not create any more of the same pattern and that he will remain content with this one example'.[10] In fact, Mr G.F. Braddock, the British Trade Commissioner in Dublin, could see 'no prospect of any real change in direction of coming to terms [. . .] so long as Mr de Valera remained in office'[11] – not so with Dominion Office officials. When Mr J.P. Walsh visited Dublin he was always welcomed by the Dominion Office, especially by Sir Harry Batterbee, the main intermediary between Dublin and Whitehall. Batterbee and his colleagues were most indulgent towards the Irish, despite W.B. Browne, Assistant Secretary at the Board of Trade's warning that 'any attempt to defend preferences to the Irish on the grounds of their Commonwealth membership might bring the whole system into controversy'.[12] The Dominion Office believed that without the same concessions as those afforded to the other Dominions, a satisfactory agreement would be very difficult. Accordingly, John Dulanty appears to have had such open access to the Dominion Office, that he was in danger of being mistaken for one of their own officials.

It was therefore only logical that when a breakthrough in the British-Irish impasse occurred in late 1937, that the initiative should have come from the Dominion Office. After years of carefully monitoring Mr de Valera's every

10 CAB 27/526, ISC (32) 86, Memorandum by Granard, 25 August 1934, PRO. 11 DO35/894/X20/2, Note by Stephenson, 2 September 1937, PRO. 12 DO35/3/99/111 11a/288 Minute by Stephenson, 28 December 1936. Quoted in McMahon, *Republicans and imperialists*, p. 201.

move and mood the Dominion Office pounced when a softening in his attitude became apparent during the Geneva meeting of the League of Nations in September 1937. Despite Board of Trade objections to quantitative concessions on imports of Irish store cattle, potatoes, eggs, poultry, and Treasury objections to a 'lump sum' which would be insufficient to cover the default, Malcolm McDonald produced his 'Prospects of Settlement of Outstanding Questions' on 14 December 1937 which was subsequently accepted by the Cabinet and became the basis for the 1938 Anglo-Irish agreement.

Similarly with Australia – Dominion Office manoeuvres at Ottawa in 1932 could have broken the August deadlock in those negotiations had Australia not given way first on meat. Again during the 1936 meat negotiations, close relations between Stanley M. Bruce, F.L. MacDougall and officials in the Dominion Office, especially N.E. Archer, paid handsome dividends. Bruce suggested to MacDonald that 'the position might be met if it were possible to arrange that while total imports from all countries taken together would not exceed total shipments for 1935, imports of beef from foreign countries should be reduced in each of the first two years by 2.5% and the Dominions should be entitled to fill the gap thus created'.[13] MacDonald, accordingly made that recommendation to the Cabinet on 22 June 1936 and it was accepted. The meat impasse had at last been broken and Australia did remarkably well. Australia had been granted an expanding share of imports, no limitation was placed on chilled exports and while a level of three farthings was imposed on foreign chilled beef imports and two thirds of a penny on foreign frozen beef imports, Dominion produce was admitted free.

In all these manoeuvres, however, the Dominion Office was reacting – reacting at Ottawa in 1932 and in London in 1936 to initiatives taken by other government departments and their ministers and in 1938 to the stalemate in the negotiations between the Irish Situation Committee in London and Mr de Valera in Dublin. The outcome in all cases was favourable to Australia and to Ireland but the process would undoubtedly have been faster, not to say smoother, had the Dominion Office been allowed to orchestrate the proceedings itself. That was of less account for the Irish than it was for the Australians. Mr de Valera never expected the Dominion Office to take the initiative in the first place; he considered that to be his own prerogative and so was not unduly concerned about which Whitehall department responded to his suggestions. He was generally unsympathetic to all Whitehall overtures. Australia, on the other hand, was often happy to defer to the Dominion Office's judge-

13 D. Machtig to G. Whiskard, 30 June 1936, DO35, 258/9105/3/99, PRO.

ment in the belief that with that department championing its cause, success would be guaranteed. It failed to notice, whether deliberately or not, that the Dominion Office could not deliver.

The most demanding test of Dominion Office officials' skill in steering their Secretary of States between the war was the Ottawa Conference in 1932. Responsibility for 'minding' J.H. Thomas, Secretary of State for Dominions, 1930–35, fell to Geoffrey Whiskard, then a junior official in the Dominion Office after the Principal Officer, Liesching, went down early with a 'sharp attack of nerves and indigestion'.[14] In a personal letter to E.H. Harding, Permanent Head of the Dominion Office in London, on 13 August, Whiskard deplored the fact that Thomas 'would not keep his mouth shut. He agreed beforehand and really and truly to lie low and to say nothing: but as soon as the discussions begins, out it all comes. I have had to shut him up at least a dozen times and he gets rather peeved; but he does shut up.'.[15] Thomas seldom objected, though on one occasion, according to Whiskard, he [Thomas] jumped down his throat and said in effect that he would have a row with whom he pleased and when he pleased, but that did not last long and Thomas was soon back in step. Whiskard could later report that 'J.H. made an admirable speech in which he said nothing very nicely'.[16] In so doing, he was complying with Whiskard's and the Dominion Office's objective of maintaining harmony within the Commonwealth. Whiskard was not unduly concerned, as he wrote himself, about whether 'a scheme would or would not work', but he was most anxious lest 'in sitting around the table and trying to make it work, the United Kingdom and the Dominions would come to blows over their respective shares'.[17]

The Dominion Office's targets were thus limited to preserving the existing balance within the Commonwealth between Britain and the Dominions and between the Dominions themselves. And at Ottawa at least, Dominion Office officials succeeded in steering Thomas along that path. Whiskard later complimented himself that the Board of Trade had been blocked from promulgating a series of 'bilateral agreements as though the Dominions concerned were a set of foreigners'.[18] But Australia, of course, wanted more – it wanted a larger share of the British market especially for its meat products even if that meant upsetting the existing balance within the Commonwealth. Its success at Ottawa, therefore, owed more to concessions from British government departments other than the Dominion Office, despite J.H. Thomas's latter day con-

14 Whiskard to Harding, 22 July 1932, DO121/61, PRO. 15 Ibid., 13 August 1932. 16 Ibid., 3 August, 1932. 17 Ibid. 18 Ibid., 5 August 1932.

version to the Australian cause. On the other hand, because the success of the Dominion Office's solution to the Irish stalemate in 1932 depended on maintaining the existing balance within the Commonwealth, it found itself with a role to play that was both palatable and advantageous to itself and that was also welcomed by the Irish delegates at the Ottawa Conference.

From the very start, even on the boat over, Whiskard held a watching brief on the Irish for the Dominion Office. He acknowledged that Sean T. O'Kelly's speech at the opening session 'was one of the most adroit performances I have ever heard', though he also noted that at the government dinner later that evening O'Kelly dissipated every bit of prestige which he had acquired at the opening ceremony by a singularly foolish speech which started in Irish, went on in English and ended in the very worst French which I have ever heard spoken in public. I do not think he was wholly responsible for his actions'.[19] That may well have endeared O'Kelly to J.H. Thomas because from then on a warm friendship developed between himself, O'Kelly and Sean Lemass, the other Irish delegate at Ottawa.

Thomas's relationship with O'Kelly and Lemass persuaded Dominion Office officials that a solution could be found to the Irish problem within an Imperial context, thereby elevating British-Irish negotiations to a place that had not been originally envisaged. The solution proposed by E.J. Harding, permanent head of the Dominion Office in London and readily accepted by Thomas was:

> at the last meeting of the Heads of delegations when we are finally settling the proposals which will be formally confirmed at the closing plenary session, Bennet speaking for Canada and supported by Bruce and Havinga, speaking for Australia and South Africa, would nominate their Chief Justice or some other Justice of the Supreme Court to examine into the validity of the financial agreement existing between us, which are the cause of the present dispute and to make a report thereon to those governments which your government would accept or not. It being understood that pending the receipt of their recommendations, there should be an economic truce between the two governments, that is, that we should revert to the status quo that existed before tarrif legislation passed by both sides.[20]

For that scheme to work it was essential that the Ottawa Conference succeed, that the Commonwealth Heads of delegations co-operate and finally, that Mr

19 Ibid., 22 July 1932. 20 File S6157A, State Paper Office, Dublin Castle.

de Valera participate. All three requirements were most doubtful. The conference was getting more and more bogged down in meat negotiations, the Commonwealth leaders had not been advised of the plan and on past evidence, Mr de Valera was hardly likely to respond to a Commonwealth initiative. J.H. Thomas, however, prompted by his Dominion Office officials, was determined to succeed, even if that entailed sacrificing traditional Labour policies. Solving the Irish problem and strengthening the Commonwealth apparently meant more to him than local British political considerations. What mattered most therefore at Ottawa, was not the months of preparation in London and Commonwealth capitals, nor was it the negotiating skills of delegates, nor was it the initial ineptness of the British delegates, but rather it was Thomas's championing of Ireland's cause, ironically, unknown to the Irish themselves. On its own, that gesture might appear insignificant, but by a remarkable coincidence, Thomas's intervention coincided with the imminent breakdown of the Australian meat negotiations and so with the possible collapse of the conference itself – a potential tragedy, especially for the Dominion Office. Prompted by Irish considerations then, Thomas proferred a life line that had it been availed of, would have conceded all the Australian demands and would have ensured that the Commonwealth survived to break the British-Irish impasse.

But this attempt to reinforce the Commonwealth failed: Australia backed down on her meat demands; Ramsay MacDonald demurred and de Valera refused Commonwealth arbitration. Thomas, Harding, Whiskard, O'Kelly and Lemass had little to show for their initiatives. The Dominion Office however, while defeated, was not daunted. As already shown, for the remainder of the decade it worked hard to maintain channels of communication between Ireland and Whitehall; it was ably abetted by the ubiquitous Dulanty whose influence was enhanced as was that of the Dominion Office itself by the accession of Malcolm McDonald to the Secretaryship of the Department. All three, as had been observed, played an important role in ending the economic war between Ireland and England in 1938. In its dealings with Ireland, the Dominion Office was also fortunate in most instances in having the Board of Trade on side which tended to offset the opposition encountered from the Treasury and from the Department of Agriculture.

This however, was not the case with Australia. Following their experience at Ottawa, most Whitehall Departments in the 1930s were antagonistic towards Australia. Sir Henry Fountain of the Board of Trade was spurred to write to Whiskard in September 1932 when the matter of further concessions in respect of pork and meat arose advising him 'not to give way too readily to the wishes of the Australians, to continue screwing concessions out of us up till the last possible moment'[21] while Mr Twentyman of the Treasury was upset that Bruce 'has been going about saying that United Kingdom officials do not know how to bargain and that it is not his job to teach them and that if they had been more alert they would have got more concessions from his government'.[22] But Ottawa was not the only cause of resentment; many departments had their own particular grievances – the Department of Agriculture found that as British agriculture had become more intensive during the 1930s it was hampered by the terms of the Ottawa Agreement and therefore that Australia was only entitled in the case of meat, to an expanding share of imports, obviously at the expense of foreigners but not at the expense of the British producer. The President of the Board of Trade argued hotly that Australia was reneging on her Ottawa commitments; he accused the Australian Tarrif Board of misinterpreting Article 10 of that Treaty and he was furious on a few occasions when the Australian government refused to impose a whip after Tariff Board reports had been presented to parliament.[23] The Lord Chancellor also had a grievance. He was apparently horrified at the request of the Tasmanian government for a say in the selection of judicial lords in the James case in 1936, the major Australian trading and market issue to reach the privy council in the 1930s. Sir Claude Schuster, head of the Lord Chancellor's office wrote that 'the Lord Chancellor was astonished and also that a private litigant would be properly committed for contempt of court in a similar situation'.[24]

The Dominion Office therefore, in promoting Australia's case and harmony within the Commonwealth was at a disadvantage. But the real tragedy was not the ineffectiveness of the Dominion Office in that respect, but rather that countries such as Australia failed to recognise that fact. Australia throughout the 30s and later continued to court the Dominion Office long after it became apparent to most except perhaps the Australians that the Dominion Office could not deliver. As a result, Australia failed to develop close contacts with other British government departments in the misguided belief that it could depend on the Dominion Office. The outcome after 1932 was far less favourable to Australia than might have been the case had Australia spread its wings more widely while still maintaining a special relationship with the Dominion Office.

21 Fountain to Whiskard, 20 September 1932, DO35, 273/9261/7, PRO. 22 Twentyman to Whiskard, 12 October 1932, DO35, 273/9261/11, PRO. 23 Board of Trade Memo, 28 April 1938 in DO35, 749/01/46, PRO. 24 Schuster to Dominion Office, 25 May 1936, DO35, 390/10892/16 PRO.

Australia's problems were compounded by the fact that when a British High Commissioner was appointed for the first time in Australia, he was drawn from the Dominion Office and unfortunately for Australia, he did not get on with his Board of Trade counterpart in Australia. Sir Geoffrey Whiskard, the High Commissioner in question, considered that the Board of Trade representative 'always looks on the dark side of things'[25] and was accordingly reluctant to consult or take him into his confidence. Eventually, E.J. Harding had to take the unusual step of cautioning his own friend and colleague, Whiskard, about his relations with Dalton, the senior Board of Trade representative in Australia – 'there would have been advantages in consultation with Dalton as Dalton had a profound knowledge of the requirements of Australia'.[26] That was correct. In trading matters, Dalton was far superior to Whiskard; he had a detailed grasp of most items of manufacture in Australia as well as a comprehensive view of the overall agricultural situation. This could not be said of Whiskard, who surprisingly seems to have considered his posting in Australia as a reward for past services and so put in a minimal amount of effort into the job: 'there really is very little work for the High Commissioner to do here', he wrote, 'it's the rarest thing in the world to go to the office in the afternoon . . . the idleness has really been a heavy burden'.[27]

He and Sir Henry Gullett, the Australian Minister for Trade Treaties, were particularly close. Whiskard wrote to Harding on the occasion of Gullett's resignation in March 1937 that he had:

> developed an increasingly warm affection for him. We have encouraged him to drop into dinner and he has probably done so a dozen times or more in the last six months [. . .] I have found him not only agreeable but really lovable.[28]

These contacts must have inevitably reinforced Gullett's expectations of the Dominion Office and confirmed his erroneous appreciation of Britain's trading policy in the 1930s. Had he been closer to Dalton, the situation might have been otherwise, but he was not. Dalton had a lowly opinion of Gullett:

> He is a difficult person, hypercritical in many things, and liable to be both strongly conceited and obstinate. His views even at present tend

25 Note on File by Whiskard, DO35/240/881H/38, PRO. **26** Harding to Whiskard, 8 July 1936, DO35, 278/9279/156, PRO. **27** Whiskard to E. Machtig (Dominion Office Official), 6 April 1941, Machtig papers. **28** Whiskard to Harding, 15 March 1937, DO35, 751/02/15, PRO.

> to be very narrow and it seems doubtful whether in fact he has ever realized that time has changed and that Australia cannot afford to continue to be as self-centred and acquisitive as she has been in the past.[29]

Being resident in Sydney, Dalton was not part of the Canberra social round so that he would have had few opportunities for socialising with Gullett or with other members of the Australian Cabinet. That may well have suited him; the loss was more Australia's than the United Kingdom's.

While the Australians courted them and while the Irish listened to them, Dominion Office officials felt assured. They worked hard to respond, relishing their intermediary role, and happy that their limitations were apparently not recognised. However, after World War II, with changes of government in Ireland and in Australia, doubts began to be expressed in both countries respecting the return on their links with the Dominion Office, now re-named the Commonwealth Relations Office. In Australia, Dr Evatt, the Labor Foreign Minister, resented British civil service involvement in Australian domestic affairs while in Ireland, the Costello government and in particular, Mr Sean MacBride, by repealing the External Relations Act, insisted that Irish-British relations should be no different from those of any other foreign country and should therefore be the responsibility of the British Foreign Office and not the Commonwealth Relations Office. These developments obviously had a devastating effect on the Commonwealth Relations Office, especially as it smelt of collusion between the two countries. From being the Irish and the Australian governments' friend at Whitehall, the Commonwealth Relations Office in a fit of more than pique tended to distance itself from its former confidantes.

Following the demise of the India Office as an independent entity in 1947, the Commonwealth Relations Office's predecessors, the Dominions Office, had been obliged to absorb the staff of that department: initially two distinct streams were retained but by 1949, the two departments had merged. That step inevitably led to frustrated career prospects for many, not only in the India Office, but even in the Dominions Office itself where it became apparent that while the middle ranks of the service had swelled, the pinnacle was as pointed as ever. Only the lucky ones could expect to advance as in the case of Sir Gilbert Laithwaite an ex-India official who became the first British ambassador to Ireland. Ireland's departure from the Commonwealth now threatened

29 Dalton to President of Board of Trade, 27 January 1932, DO35, 240/8831H/10, PRO. **30** Memo by J. Garner, 15 August 1950, DO35/3984A, PRO.

the Commonwealth Relations Office itself; it only had a rationale while a Commonwealth existed. Commonwealth Relations Office officials were fighting as much for their own survival as for the Commonwealth itself. This fear was not imaginary. MacBride expected that once the External Relations Act was repealed 'control of relations with the Irish Republic would be handed over to the Foreign Office'. But even more disturbing for them was the suggestion by Dr Evatt that the Commonwealth Relations Office should be abolished. Following MacBride's note, the Commonwealth Relations Office became convinced:

> If Ireland was to go to the Foreign Office, it would set a bad example to three new Dominions who are already inclined to vie with one another in eliminating any marks of Commonwealth relationship. It would also strengthen those elements in the old Dominions such as Dr Evatt and Dr Burton who advocate that the Commonwealth Relations Office should be transferred to the Foreign Office and encourage the Foreign Office themselves to resume, in spite of their setback, their intrigues for absorbing into their Empire the whole field of Commonwealth Relations.[31]

As a result, the Irish government could no longer count on the support of the Commonwealth Relations Office. As has been seen in the 1930s, the Dominion Office had championed the Irish case in the face of hostilities from other government departments. Norman Archer was one such official but by 1948, he had become noticeably soured. Writing to Sir Norman Brooke in December 1948, he remarked that the 'underlying difficulty is that while views in Whitehall are formed on a basis of reason and commonsense, it has been my difficult duty to represent that this approach may be inapplicable to Éire'.[32] A similar transformation is noticeable in the attitude of Gordon Walker, a government minister at the Commonwealth Relations Office. He had been alone in an attempt to tone down the initial response of the Commonwealth Relations Office to Ireland's decision to repeal the ERA – later, however, he was adamant that the Unionists in Northern Ireland should be wholeheartedly accommodated even if it meant further alienating the Eire government. In a note to Attlee in January 1949, he wrote: 'I am in favour of standing up to Eire

31 Memo from Commonwealth Relations Office to Secretary of State for Commonwealth Relations, undated, but presumably August 1950, DO35/3984A, PRO. **32** Norman Archer to Sir Norman Brook, 23 December 1948, DO35/3968, PRO.

if necessary over the guarantee of Northern Ireland's continuation as an integral part of the United Kingdom',[33] and he also revealed that they, at the Commonwealth Relations Office, would have gone further in meeting with Sir Basil Brooke's requirements had other departments not raised specific technical objections.

Thus Dominion Office loyalty was conditional; conditional on whatever ensured its own survival. But within that wide spectrum it played an important part in cementing Commonwealth relations. It was not its fault if countries like Australia exaggerated the department's importance or if countries like Ireland rejected its initiatives – what was remarkable was that the office could maintain cohesion for so long within so amorphous a body as the British Commonwealth. Its own survival instincts had therefore positive results and it is surely not surprising then that its decline and eventual absorption within the Foreign Office coincided with the erosion of the Commonwealth itself. By then, Australia had realised that Commonwealth cohesion alone fell short of its expectations of the Dominion Office. What is remarkable is that it had taken so long and that despite repeated reverses, Australia had not demurred. The Irish expected less, so that even minor advances were considered bonuses and Dominion Office involvement, while welcomed, was not considered imperative. Thus the mutual satisfaction of the interests of the three was narrowly confined so that the frequency and range of their exchanges were not matched by corresponding returns.

33 Gordon Walker's comments on Sir Norman Brook's Working Party Report on the measures required following the report of the External Relations Act, January 1949. DO130/105, PRO.

7

Ireland's departure from the British Commonwealth

Ever since John A. Costello, the Irish Prime Minister, announced in Canada on 7 September 1948 that his government was going to repeal the External Relations Act, that decision has been shrouded in controversy. Costello himself always maintained that it was a deliberate decision of the government and that his announcement in Canada was due to a leak in the *Sunday Independent* on 5 September about the intention of the Irish Government. He has been supported in that claim by his Minister for External Affairs Seán MacBride, while on the other hand his Minister for Health, Dr Noel Browne has alleged that it was an impulsive move provoked by the reception which Costello received in Canada, especially the placing of a silver replica of 'Roaring Meg', the famous canon used by the Protestants in their defence of Derry's walls against the Catholics, in front of him at dinner. In fact, Browne goes further and states that Costello proffered his resignation on his return because 'he had no authority from the Cabinet for his decision' although other Cabinet members, for example, James Dillon, Dan Morrissey and Paddy McGilligan denied that any such Cabinet meeting ever took place.[1]

It is obviously impossible to reconcile such irreconcilable positions, but I hope in this article to draw some conclusions, based on a detailed analysis of the crucial events of late 1948 and early 1949, which place those events in a clearer relief. This analysis surprisingly uncovers another participant in the saga, namely Dr H.V. Evatt, the Australian Deputy Prime Minister and Minister for External Affairs who, without any prompting from the Irish, played a vital role in averting a hostile response by the British to Costello's move. Dr Evatt's motives are as obscure as Costello's. He had no previous involvement in Irish internal affairs; he was not of Irish extraction and he had no instructions from Canberra, but he was destined to play a pivotal part in the crisis.

In repealing the External Relations Act (ERA) the Costello government had two objectives in mind – first to break the last connection with the British

1 Ronan Fanning, *Independent Ireland* (1983), pp. 172–80; Noel Browne, *Against the tide* (1980), pp. 129–33.

Crown and second to confirm Ireland's departure from the British Commonwealth. While under the terms of the 1926 Balfour Declaration and the subsequent Statute of Westminster these two steps were inextricably linked, the Commonwealth had undergone profound changes in the intervening years. For example, appeals to the Privy Council were being abolished, Commonwealth countries were acquiring full powers of constitutional amendment and they also now had direct access to the Crown. The Commonwealth itself therefore was changing, especially in its relationship with Britain and with the King so that even within the British civil service doubts were being raised about the durability of the link.

Neil Pritchard, a Commonwealth Relations officer, seconded to the office of the British representative in Dublin 1948, held that 'if the crucial issue in the present concept of the Commonwealth is represented by the tenuous link with the Crown incorporated in the External Relations Act, it is difficult to see why we should regard the Commonwealth idea as worth defending. If we accept neutrality as being possible within the Commonwealth – why should we jib at a republic?'[2] In a similar vein, Dr Herbert V. Evatt, the Australian Deputy Prime Minister, urged that they should not hesitate 'to explore any of the possibilities of new modes, forms or symbols of association which may be suggested even if they were to depart in some respects from the orthodoxy of the Balfour Report'.[3] The monarch was therefore becoming dispensible for the Commonwealth so that a break with the Crown need not necessarily imply a break with the Commonwealth.

The Éire government, however, could not envisage a Commonwealth without a king – the Indian expedient in which the monarch was symbolic of the link between countries rather than the head of their association, was unacceptable to the Costello government. And even if it had been possible for them to exorcize the monarch from the Commonwealth it is doubtful if they would have renewed their membership; in their view, the Commonwealth being the offspring of the British Empire was still a testimony to servitude and compulsion rather than an ongoing guarantor of basic freedoms and they accordingly rejected it. In fact they went even further and insisted that they had left the Commonwealth in 1936. By insisting on a republic outside of the Commonwealth, Ireland forfeited whatever chance it might have had of salvaging some of its former Commonwealth benefits. At a meeting which Sir Norman Brook, Secretary to the British Cabinet, had with the Prime Ministers of Aus-

2 Memo from Neil Pritchard, 8 September 1948, DO 35/3960, PRO 3 Letter from H.V. Evatt to C. Attlee, 12 October 1948, DO 35/3962, PRO.

tralia, Canada and New Zealand about the end of August 1948 the 'general feeling among them was that if the ERA was repealed, they had no alternative but to regard Éire as a foreign country'.[4]

Britain could now either extend all Éire's former privileges to other foreign countries or else they could strip Éire of them and place her on a similar footing to existing foreigners. She initially opted for the latter, on the grounds of the impracticability of the former course but also because her attitude towards Ireland began to harden once it became apparent that Ireland wanted neither the King nor the Commonwealth. A punitive element now crept into their response and within a short time they became obdurate in their resistance to any concessions to the Irish. Unfortunately for the Irish, this coincided with a fear about its own future, then rampant within the Commonwealth Relations Office (CRO) itself.

Dispatches from Lord Rugby, the British representative in Dublin tended to reinforce hostility. Rugby appears to have had a lowly opinion of the Costello government, especially of Costello himself: the fact that Costello failed to recognize this and made a unique presentation (eighteen silver bacon dishes and four silver salt-cellars) to Rugby on his departure for his 'signal assistance to both Britain and Ireland',[5] must have reassured Rugby in his assessment of Costello. In a letter to Sir Eric Machtig, permanent head of the Commonwealth Relations Office, Rugby wrote that 'Mr. Costello personally had conducted this business in a slapdash and amateur fashion'. Rugby also detected signs of uneasiness in the department of External Affairs at Mr Costello's incautious remarks'[6] and he even advised the Commonwealth Relations Office to cultivate MacBride in order to win his assistance in containing Costello's republican proclivities.[7] Rugby was also relieved that Costello declined Attlee's invitation to discuss the repeal of the ERA with himself and Commonwealth leaders in October 1948 and he was pleased that MacBride attended in his place because Rugby believed that 'Mr Costello was so "emotional" on that question that he cannot easily be made to look at the facts – Mr MacBride would be more calm'.[8] This constant stream of anti Costello reports could only further alienate the CRO and sharpen the existing divisions between Ireland and Britain.

Ireland's actions did little to mitigate that antagonism; if anything, they accentuated it though it is doubtful if the Irish government fully realized the

4 Report by Sir Charles Dixon on the 'Departure of Éire from the British Commonwealth of Nations', DO 35/3979, PRO. 5 Neil Pritchard to Sir Percival Liesching on Lord Rugby's departure DO 35/3970, PRO. 6 Lord Rugby to CRO, 25 November 1948, DO 35/3963, PRO. 7 N.E. Archer to the Secretary of State for Commonwealth Relations, undated, DO 35/3936, PRO. 8 Memo from CRO to Attlee, 13 October 1948, DO 35/3962, PRO.

dangers inherent in the line it was taking. Their expectations of Attlee, their confidence in other Commonwealth leaders and their disregard for possible legal difficulties lured them into a false sense of security that only strengthened their resolve to pursue their set course. MacBride made absolutely clear to Lord Rugby from the outset that in order 'to avoid any risk of misunderstanding, its decision to repeal the ERA was not open to revision or modification'.[9] Their mistaken trust in Attlee was based primarily on personal friendship but also his lack of response up till then, to developments in Ireland, bred a false complacency. Attlee was admittedly on very friendly terms with MacBride and in fact had toured Mayo by car in the company of Mr and Mrs MacBride in the summer of 1948. MacBride understandably believed that he enjoyed Attlee's confidence. Further, both Noel Baker, the Secretary of State for Commonwealth relations and the Lord Chancellor, Lord Jowitt, visited Ireland that year and in fact the Lord Chancellor had toasted the President of Ireland at an official dinner (in the Royal Dublin Society) without any rebuke from Attlee.[10] But Attlee was much more attuned to Sir Basil Brooke's overtures than he was to MacBride's, no doubt conscious of Northern Ireland's role in the recent war. It was Attlee himself who inserted the parliamentary guarantee to the Northern Ireland Unionists in the 1949 Ireland Act, contrary to the recommendations of his working party.[11] And he recommended the withdrawal of citizenship rights and trading preferences from the Irish in the event of a repeal of the ERA.[12] However, the Costello government was not to know.

Second, they expected support from Commonwealth countries without obtaining any prior assurances and while this did eventually materialize, it could not have been foreseen or taken for granted. The only intimation which the Costello government had of Commonwealth assistance prior to their announcement of the repeal of the ERA came from MacKenzie King. Costello acknowledged that fact in the Dáil[13] and Rugby deplored the 'dangerous encouragement during Costello's visit to Canada'. MacKenzie King was alone in proffering that encouragement as there is no evidence to suggest that the Costello government had obtained the backing of other Commonwealth governments prior to September 1948; on the contrary, as has been noted, Commonwealth Ministers in London in August 1948 had agreed with Sir Norman Brooke following the repeal of the ERA, that Éire should be treated as a for-

9 Lord Rugby to CRO, 12 October 1948 in which he reported a conversation he had with Mac Bride. DO 35/3960, PRO. **10** Lord Rugby to Sir Eric Machtig, 1 December 1948, DO 35/3969, PRO. **11** Cabinet Paper, 10 January 1949. CAB 129/32, Part 1. **12** Revised draft of note to the Éire government, 12 November 1948, DO 35/3964, PRO. **13** Costello's Dáil speech, 25 November 1948 on the second reading of the repeal of the External Relations Act.

eign country.[14] Even Dr Evatt, who was later to play such a prominent role in averting that outcome, was apparently stunned when he heard of Costello's intention. By a strange coincidence both Dr Evatt and P.J. Noel Baker were in Dublin on 7 September 1948 when Costello made his speech in Canada. Noel Baker reported that 'they were both taken completely by surprise and Dr Evatt was extremely indignant. He said it had placed him in a most difficult position as a guest of the Éire government.'[15] It would therefore seem that MacKenzie King's support was sufficient for the Éire government.

One final, and perhaps unusual feature of the Irish refusal to compromise was their disregard for the legal difficulties inherent in their proposals. Éire Ministers told A.P. Ryan of *The Times* of London that as 'they were all lawyers themselves, they knew very well that there were always ways around legal difficulties'.[16] After the Chequers meeting in October 1948, MacBride told Lord Rugby that 'none of the questions raised presented a difficulty which lawyers could not get around',[17] though Rugby also added that 'Boland (Secretary of Irish Department of External Affairs) seemed less ready to brush aside the possible difficulties'. And after the Paris talks in November 1948, MacBride again told Rugby that he was 'not worried' about legal difficulties which he alleged the 'British exaggerated' using them 'to oppose political change'.[18] On the other hand, Boland indicated that the legal problems 'had not penetrated the minds of the Éire Ministers'.[19]

It is therefore apparent that Ireland's determination to proceed with the repeal of the External Relations Act without regard to possible adverse repercussions, was based on ill conceived hypotheses: Mr Attlee turned out to be a hostile witness; the Commonwealth was at best tepid and at worst hostile to Éire while nearly all lawyers in both Ireland and England with the exception of those in the Costello cabinet, insisted that the legal difficulties were considerable. Britain was not likely to make any concessions; she believed she had the Commonwealth behind her; she was convinced that the Irish proposal was ridden with legal flaws; she was bespoken to the Unionists to protect their status within the UK and the CRO had its own peculiar reasons for opposing change. On balance then, there is little doubt that unless some unforeseen developments took place, Costello's decision to repeal the External Relations Act would have adversely affected Irish citizens abroad and Irish trade. This

14 Lord Rugby to CRO, 25 November 1948, DO 35/3963, PRO. **15** Note by P.J. Noel Baker, 27 May 1948, DO 103/104, PRO. **16** Neil Pritchard to N.E. Archer, 11 November 1948, DO 35/3964, PRO. **17** Lord Rugby to Sir Eric Machtig, 19 October 1948, DO 35/3961, PRO. **18** Lord Rugby to CRO, 19 November 1948, DO 35/3964, PRO. **19** Lord Rugby to CRO, 11 November 1948, DO 35/3964, PRO.

of course ignores the role played by Dr Evatt in the proceedings, but in September 1948 the British could be excused for taking his cooperation for granted. Chifley, the Australian Prime Minister, had pledged support for Britain in August and Dr Evatt was 'extremely indignant' at Costello's announcement. It therefore came as a great shock to the British when Dr Evatt decided to champion the Irish cause from October onwards.

The British liked to think that Evatt's conversion to the Irish cause was inspired by electoral considerations in Victoria. There may be some truth in this though it is unusual that Chifley, the Prime Minister, was not unduly concerned about the Irish vote in Victoria and Evatt himself, being an MP for a Sydney constituency, had little to fear personally from the Irish in Victoria, whose numbers anyway were declining. Of possibly greater importance for Evatt was his concern for world peace-keeping bodies – he had been largely instrumental in designing the Charter for the United Nations and in 1948, he was President of that body. He was equally committed to the British Commonwealth as a vehicle for the preservation of peace and of the democratic way of life in the world and so he was loath to see it being undermined or fragmented. In his opinion the departure of Ireland was a significant step in that direction especially as Ireland in his view was as much a mother country as Britain. Evatt, however, was less concerned with structures than with the essentials of the Commonwealth community believing that 'legal conceptions must be adopted to fit the facts of the long established and close historical connections between Éire and the UK',[20] rather than vice versa. And in his letter of 12 October to Attlee, he advised that they should 'avoid at this stage formulating conditions which must be accepted in order that a particular state shall not cease to be a member of the Commonwealth' and he recommended that they should look into the possibility of 'finding links that would be acceptable to all, including Ireland'.[21] It was for the Commonwealth to make the adjustment and not Éire.

In this respect he appears to have been acting entirely on his own initiative. Archie Cameron MHR for Barker, asked Chifley if 'relations between Australia and Éire were left entirely to the discretion of our wandering star in Paris' – the Prime Minister replied that they were not and that 'Australian government policy had been perfectly clear for a considerable time' and that 'he had made that clear at the Conference of Empire ministers'.[22] He did not

20 Letter from Ian Mac Lennon to British High Commissioners in Commonwealth countries, 10 December 1948. DO 35/3965, PRO. **21** H. V. Evatt to C. Attlee, 12 October 1948, DO 35/3962, PRO. **22** Telegram from Acting British High Commissioner in Canberra to CRO, 25 November 1948. DO 35/3965, PRO.

say what that policy was but when pressed the following day, again in the House of Representatives, he reiterated Australia's own view of the Commonwealth which was based 'upon our relations with the King not merely as a symbol of association but as our monarch and enjoying the same loyalty and affection in Australia as in Britain itself – not only for the King but for the Royal family',[23] thereby anticipating Menzies' famous Adelaide speech in which he referred to those in the old dominions as being 'the king's subjects and the king's men'.[24] Evatt's Commonwealth was much more widely based; it had room for much more than the 'king's men' and because of that he could promote Ireland's interests, seemingly impervious to the views of his Prime Minister or his Cabinet colleagues. It would also appear that Evatt failed to keep the Cabinet informed of developments. A detailed search in Canberra of all the communications from overseas received in the Department of External Affairs during that period has failed to unearth any from Dr Evatt. It was only after a settlement had been reached in Paris in November 1948 that J.A. Beasley, the Australian High Commissioner in London, informed Chifley of the outcome, extolling the role of 'the Doc' in the process.[25]

Evatt's effectiveness was enhanced by the fact that he was in Europe and not in Canberra because it is extremely doubtful if he would have received the backing of the Cabinet for his actions. Equally important was the presence in Paris of both the New Zealand Prime Minister, Peter Fraser, and of the Canadian Secretary of State for External Affairs, Lester Pearson. Whilst not as committed as Evatt to Éire's case, they became staunch allies, under Evatt's tutelage, and gave him their full backing at the Paris meeting in November. Again it is doubtful if these two Commonwealth statesmen would have carried their cabinets with them on the issue had they not been away from home; being abroad they had far greater leeway because instead of having to obtain prior approval for their actions, they found it possible to present their colleagues with a fait accompli, making it very difficult for the latter to withhold their endorsement. However, in spite of that, the arrangements did come very near to being unstuck in both New Zealand and Canada. Meeting on 24 November in Pearson's absence, the Canadian Cabinet was 'very cold towards Éire' and was angry that such important matters were being dealt with in 'unseemly haste due to the Irish pressure' and so they refused to make a state-

23 Telegram from Acting UK High Commissioner in Canberra to the CRO, 26 November 1948. DO 35/3965, PRO. 24 *The British Commonwealth of Nations in International Affairs* (1950), p. 3. 25 A 3830, 1948, IK 18352, Australian Archives, Canberra (AA). According to Beasley: 'Only for the doc and he was supported by Fraser and Pearson, the Conference would have bogged down and the obstinacy of both sides left further memories'.

ment welcoming the course taken at Paris.[26] It required Mr Pearson's presence, on his return, to rescue the situation.[27] The New Zealand Cabinet, in Mr Fraser's absence, was also quite tepid in its response, concluding that 'there must be serious doubts whether the policy proposed is tenable'. However, after hearing from Fraser, they modified their view saying that arrangements would create more problems for the UK than for New Zealand. Ireland could also depend on Luow from South Africa for support though because of the small numbers of Irish in South Africa, he did not participate in the actual negotiation. Thus, the presence of Evatt, of Fraser and Pearson in Paris was of signal importance for the Irish. Without them it is doubtful if the Irish would have made any headway with the British.

Dr Evatt and his Commonwealth colleagues had less success with the Irish than with the British. The Irish failed to respond to any of Evatt's overtures and while at Chequers on 17 October 1948, they weakly hinted that they might consider rejoining the Commonwealth at a later stage.[28] On returning to Dublin they promptly dropped the idea and never raised it again. Even on the matter of reciprocal privileges for Irish and Commonwealth citizens in the other person's country, the Irish refused to match like for like. The British, on the other hand, were much more amenable to Dr Evatt's overtures – not because they were convinced of the merits of his case but rather because they placed Commonwealth solidarity before the inevitable hostile foreign reaction to the Éire settlement. The British Cabinet decided that 'Éire should not leave the Commonwealth in circumstances that would leave a lasting grievance among other countries.'[29] It was this very leverage, used to great effect by Dr Evatt, that was to break the deadlock caused by the initial hostility of Britain to Éire's decision to repeal the ERA and Ireland's obduracy in refusing to make any concession whatsoever. Dr Evatt's greatest achievement was that he succeeded in forging an informal link between Ireland and the Commonwealth by means of the concession of non-alien status for Irish citizens in Britain and Commonwealth countries and also by allowing Ireland to retain its most favoured nation status in trade.

Britain's hard line response to Éire found expression in its draft note to the Éire Government adopted by the Cabinet on 12 November 1948. This was a

26 Letter from UK High Commissioner in Canada to the CRO, 24 November 1948, DO 35/3965, PRO. **27** F.E. Cumming Bruce to Sir Eric Machtig, 1 December 1948 where he mentions that Pearson stated that the Canadian response was substantially more forthcoming than earlier reports might suggest, DO 35/3965, PRO. **28** Telegram from UK High Commissioner in New Zealand to CRO, 24 November 1948, DO 35/3965, PRO. **29** Extract of conclusions of Cabinet meeting, 13 November 1948, DO 35/3964, PRO.

reply to an aide-memoire of 20 October from the Éire Government. In its note the British Government indicated that

> if Éire became a foreign state, any attempt to treat Éire citizens in the United Kingdom otherwise than as aliens might provoke demands from the numerous foreign countries under their treaties with the United Kingdom that their nations should enjoy similar privileges in the United Kingdom. If such demands were conceded, it would be impossible to operate in anything like its present form the whole of the United Kingdom systems of alien control. The United Kingdom government would therefore have no alternative but to bring Éire citizens under the ordinary aliens control applicable to foreign nationals.

Similarly in respect to trade the note pointed to the large number of foreign countries in which Britain had

> undertaken to accord to those countries treatment not less favourable than that accorded to any other foreign country. If Éire became a foreign state, such countries could claim that they should be treated not less favourably than Éire. The United Kingdom would therefore either have to withdraw trade preferences which she now accords to Éire; if she made no change in her treatment of Éire, the consequence would be that, except for a few protective and revenue duties, the United Kingdom government would have virtually no tariff, because every important country would have to be granted the almost universal free entry now enjoyed by Éire. For these reasons it would be difficult to avoid the consequences that the United Kingdom would be compelled to take action to terminate its commitments to accord preferential treatment in custom matters to Éire goods.[30]

This note was the outcome of weeks of deliberation during which the Commonwealth Relations Office produced the original draft; the Lord Chancellor and the Attorney General made some modifications and the Home Office also had an input before the document was finally endorsed by the Cabinet on 12 November 1948. As such it was a deliberate statement of British government policy on the repeal of the External Relations Act. It was never

30 Revised Draft of Note to the Éire Government, adopted by Cabinet on 12 November 1948, DO 35/3964, PRO.

sent. Dr Evatt's intervention prevented the government from proceeding with its intentions. Evatt accused the British of 'trying to force Éire out of the Commonwealth from the outset'[31] and Attlee felt obliged to reconsider his position.

Evatt was upset not only because of the tone of the note but also because it seemed to him to go counter to the decisions reached at an earlier conference held at Chequers. Evatt correctly took credit for that meeting; he had been instrumental in having it called – Attlee had been forced to involve other Commonwealth governments in the Irish problem against his own wishes. Rugby had advised against such a course[32] on the ground that Éire might manipulate these countries to its own advantage and in fact Machtig was later to inform his Secretary of State that 'the Irish – relied greatly on Mr Luow and Dr Evatt for sympathy and support for the Irish view of the decision to repeal the ERA'.[33] However, Attlee had little choice when Evatt took the initiative himself on 12 October 1948 and requested Attlee to convene a meeting between Commonwealth statesmen and the Éire government.[34] There is no evidence to suggest that this intervention was inspired by Dublin.

The Chequers meeting[35] was a success for Evatt; it was agreed that 'it was the wish of both Éire and Commonwealth countries that Éire and Commonwealth countries should not become foreign countries in relation to each other and that Éire citizens should not become aliens under the laws of Commonwealth countries'.[36] That was sufficient link for Evatt to retain Éire's association with the Commonwealth; but the Conference went further and apparently obtained the qualified consent of the Éire delegates that Ireland would reapply for admittance to the Commonwealth within six months. While this stipulation was not included in the subsequent exchange of notes between prime ministers and while Sir Charles Dixon in his account of the meeting merely refers to the 'possibility that Éire might, after an interval, re-enter the Commonwealth on some basis (e.g. common citizenship),[37] the detailed account of the Chequers deliberations compiled by Sir Eric Machtig and Sir Norman Brooke and later confirmed by W.E. Beckett of the Foreign Office, lays special emphasis on that aspect of the alleged agreement. The officials concluded that

31 Sir Norman Brook to C. Attlee, 12 October 1948, DO 35/3964, PRO. 32 Lord Rugby to CRO, 12 October 1948, DO 35/3960, PRO. 33 Sir Eric Machtig to Secretary of State for Commonwealth Relations, 15 October 1948, DO 35/3962, PRO. 34 H.V. Evatt to C. Attlee, 12 October 1948, DO 35/3962, PRO. 35 This meeting was held on 17 October 1948 and was confined to ministers representing the British, Irish, Canadian, Australian and New Zealand governments. Officials were not present. 36 Exchange of notes between the UK Prime Minister, representing the Prime Ministers of the Commonwealth, and the Prime Minister of Éire, DO 35/3961, PRO.

they would then 'be confronted with a new kind of Commonwealth relationship' i.e. a relationship without the King. It was also their understanding that the status quo was being maintained 'on the assumption that Éire would carry out stage two and do so within a reasonable period'.[38]

Éire chose to ignore that particular commitment and instead in its aide-memoire of 20 October, i.e. three days after the conference, laid more stress on its claim to privileged treatment which in its view was 'dependent upon long established custom or tradition and did not therefore involve the creation of new rights and privileges entitling other nations to raise objections'.[39] No mention was made of reciprocal rights between Éire and Commonwealth countries; no mention was made of re-entry – merely the retention of the status quo as of right. Britain regarded this response as a breach of trust and immediately set in motion the series of departmental discussions which resulted in the Cabinet document of 12 November 1948, in which, as has already been seen, Britain was determined to have Irish citizens in Britain treated as aliens and to withdraw all preferences for Éire under the most favoured nation clauses of trade treaties.

Dr Evatt responded differently; no doubt he was also disappointed with the Éire aide-memoire but he was equally determined that the bridge between Éire and the Commonwealth, however flimsy it might appear, should not be jettisoned. He saw in the British response a deliberate attack on Éire's membership of the Commonwealth and it confirmed him in his view that in fact Britain was trying to force Éire out. He had been equally incensed when the British, against the expressed wishes of the other ministers, had informally briefed a select band of journalists after the Chequers meeting on 'the grave consequences which would follow' for Éire if she repealed the ERA.[40] Evatt had protested that not only was this at variance with the spirit of that meeting but also that 'it had prejudiced any chance of reaching a satisfactory understanding with the Éire government'.[41] In his opinion the 12 November note was another manifestation of that mentality. There is also no evidence to suggest that he was prompted by Dublin. In the first place, the Éire government

37 Report by Sir Charles Dixon on the 'Departure of Éire from the British Commonwealth of Nations', DO 35/3979, PRO. 38 Sir Norman Brook and Sir Eric Machtig to Prime Minister, 18 October 1948, DO 35/3962, PRO. 39 This aide-memoire dated 20 October 1948 is to be found in DO 35/3964, PRO. 40 N.E. Archer to Mr Gordon Walker in which he advised that the official communique should be brief but that 'a small group of journalists should be informed of the possible consequences of Éire repealing the ERA', DO 35/3962, PRO. See also telegram to UK High Commissioners in Commonwealth countries giving detailed information about that press briefing. 41 Sir Norman Brook to Attlee, 12 November 1948, DO 35/3964, PRO.

did not anticipate such a response and so had no knowledge of the note; in fact MacBride was most surprised when the present writer informed him of it in 1983.[42] Further, Dr Evatt was hardly one to champion a cause unless he was totally committed to it himself and finally, at the end of the day after the British had capitulated, Dr Evatt, hardly the most modest of men, insisted that the British government give him full credit for it.[43]

Still in spite of that forewarning, the vehemence of Dr Evatt's reaction to the British note took all concerned by surprise; the note was delivered to Evatt in Paris by the Attorney General on the evening of 12 November; the Attorney General rang Attlee at 10.00 p.m. complaining that 'Evatt was most difficult'. Evatt would not endorse the note because he maintained 'that the consequences described in it would not follow upon Éire's repeal of the ERA – because Éire was covered by Sections 2 and 3 of the British 1948 Nationality Act' so that the 'United Kingdom would have to repeal these two sections' if Éire was to forfeit her privileges in Britain.[44] Evatt also dissociated himself from the British move and insisted that any reference to the Chequers meeting where a consensus had been achieved would have to be deleted. He also recommended that further meetings be held with Éire ministers. The Attorney General rang Attlee again at midnight to say that Fraser agreed with Evatt and that Pearson, while more reasonable, had also concurred. As a result a Cabinet meeting was hastily convened on the following morning, Saturday, 13 November,[45] at which it was decided to scrap the note to Éire and to substitute a much milder version in which they referred in vague terms to the difficulties involved in the repeal but that the 'last thing they would wish would be to be hurried into taking action in advance' and they requested that Éire government to at least delay the 'commencement of the Act'.[46] The Cabinet also agreed to reconvene a meeting of Commonwealth ministers and possibly have the Irish along as well.

Evatt once again dominated proceedings at the Paris meetings held on 14 and 16 November 1948 and it was his intervention at the opportune moment which broke the deadlock between Britain and Ireland. MacBride and MacGilligan, Ireland's Minister for Finance, representing Costello, held to their earlier position and insisted that Ireland had not been a member of the

42 Interview which writer had with Mac Bride on 28 June 1983. 43 Note by Ian Mac Lennan on 23 November 1948 of a conversation which Cumming Bruce had with Dr Evatt, DO 35/3965, PRO. 44 Sir Norman Brook to Attlee, 12 November 1948, DO 35/3964, PRO. 45 Extract of conclusions of Cabinet meeting, 13 November 1948, DO 35/3964, PRO. 46 British government reply to Éire aide-memoire, 13 November 1948, DO 35/3964, PRO.

Commonwealth since 1936, and had no intention of becoming one now. At the same time the Éire ministers 'stressed the desire of their government to continue and to strengthen the close factual relationship between Éire and the other countries of the Commonwealth.'[47] However, the British failed to see how this could be done without recourse to an unambiguous legal framework that was essential if the relations between Éire and the Commonwealth were to be consolidated – such a framework, in their view, was only feasible within the context of the Statute of Westminster.

It was at this junction that Dr Evatt made his decisive intervention. He argued that even if Éire 'was not a member of the Commonwealth, she and the Commonwealth countries would not regard one another as "foreign".' He said that 'it was a fact that an Australian would never think of himself as a foreigner in Éire any more than an Irishman would think of himself as a foreigner in Australia'[48] and later that afternoon he produced a formula encapsulating that sentiment which he hoped would prove the basis for a statement by the Éire government in the course of the debate on the second reading of the Bill to repeal the ERA. He said that 'the facts not only negative the view that Ireland and the United Kingdom, Canada, Australia and New Zealand are to be regarded as "foreign countries", but they also evidence the fact of a special association which it is the firm desire and intention of Ireland to maintain and strengthen'.[49] This formula found acceptance with MacBride – in fact he may have had an input though he does not remember; it was also acceptable to the other Commonwealth statesmen and the British eventually concurred, albeit unwillingly, because as Lord Jowitt put it, 'if we persisted in the view that Éire must be regarded as a foreign country once the ERA was repealed, we should find ourselves alone in maintaining that view'.[50] All that remained then was to work out the details and it was in these discussions that MacBride obtained a most vital concession.

Evatt's formula referred to Commonwealth citizens in Ireland being entitled to the 'rights and privileges of citizens of Ireland' but in the course of these later discussions MacBride succeeded in obtaining agreement for the exchange of 'comparable' rights as distinct from 'identical' rights. The legal background of the Costello Cabinet had some use after all! MacBride cited Ireland's constitution as an impediment to certain concessions though he did

47 Memorandum by the Lord Chancellor and the Secretary of State for Commonwealth, 17 November 1948, CAB 129/31. 48 Ibid. 49 Appendix II to Annex B – Draft Declaration, CAB 129/31,. 50 Memorandum by the Lord Chancellor and the Secretary of State for Commonwealth, 17 November 1948, CAB 129/31.

promise to review the matter in due course.[51] This limitation, however, meant what while Irish citizens enjoyed the franchise in the UK and Commonwealth citizens in Ireland; further UK and Commonwealth citizens could not serve on juries in Ireland while the restrictions imposed by the Control of Manufactures Act 1934 and the Civil Service Regulation Acts 1924 and 1927 continued unimpaired.[52]

Ireland was now of the Commonwealth without being in it. The *Sydney Sunday Sun* described it as 'so typically Irish that perhaps a solution should best be left to the Irish. No other people could hope to understand it'.[53] The *Sydney Morning Herald* commented on the fact that Attlee and Chiefley's explanation of the Repeal were so similar, and that paper correctly surmised that it was the result of 'concerted policy',[54] but the paper also observed that because 'both were obscure' it appeared that 'the immediate parties to that queer arrangement were themselves unsure of what it meant or where it would lead'. Indeed the politicians at the Paris meeting agreed that the Éire government should avoid saying anything 'which would increase the legal and political difficulties which Commonwealth governments will find in explaining the position – and Commonwealth governments will refrain from any public statements which would make it more difficult for them to maintain that despite the repeal of the ERA, Éire is not a foreign country'.[55] Boland had even recommended to Pritchard 'that in general terms the same lie should be told on both sides of the Channel'.[56] Still it suited the Irish; while the exercise was more symbolic than real it achieved their immediate objective of breaking the link with the Crown which in MacBride's opinion 'placed our relationship with Britain and other Commonwealth countries on a new and better footing on the basis of frank and cordial friendship'.[57] The Lord Chancellor in the House of Lords on 15 December might outline with due gravity the great loss to Ireland of Commonwealth membership but on closer examination, these losses appear quite trivial: Lord Jowitt singled out the 'flow and interchange of communications and the sharing of common tasks and common friends' as the 'hallmark of the Commonwealth relationship' – 'From all these things' he said 'Éire must now be exclud-

51 Note of a meeting in the offices of the Right Hon. H.V. Evatt at the Palais de Chaillot, Paris, 16 November 1948 at 5.00 p.m., CAB 129/31. 52 Report of talk which Neil Pritchard had with R. Boland, 8 December 1948, DO 35/3937, PRO. 53 Telegram from the UK High Commissioner in Canberra to CRO, 8 December 1948, DO 35/3965, PRO. 54 *Sydney Morning Herald*, 27 November 1948. 55 Memorandum by the Lord Chancellor and the Secretary of State for Commonwealth, 17 November 1948, CAB 129/31. 56 Neil Pritchard to N.E. Archer, 7 November 1948, DO 35/3961, PRO. 57 'Why Éire has cut the link with the Crown', *Sydney Morning Herald*, 29 November 1948.

ed'.[58] He was not quite correct; at a meeting on 7 January between Boland and Sir Percival Liesching, the new permanent Head of the CRO, and other UK officials it was explained to Mr. Boland that 'while Éire should go off the Committees at once' in order to mark her break with the Commonwealth, 'subsequent special ad hoc arrangements for Éire's attendance as observers were not ruled out'.[59] So that even in what was considered the most substantial of Ireland's losses, the deprivation was to be only temporary.

But there was a sting in the tail for the Irish: in claiming that she had left the Commonwealth in 1936, Ireland created doubts in the minds of legal experts in Britain about whether the 1948 British Nationality Act would apply to those arriving from Ireland. The Lord Chancellor argued that it did not apply, while Lord Simon and Sergeant Sullivan took the opposite view. In order to clear up this uncertainty, the British government decided to introduce an Ireland Bill which would place beyond doubt the status of Irish citizens in Britain.[60] Evatt had stated in November that such a Bill was superfluous[61] but he did not reckon with the line of argument which the Irish were to pursue so tenaciously. As a result the British Ireland Bill was introduced, more by accident than by design. Had the Éire government not forced it on the British government it is doubtful if they would have introduced an Ireland Bill themselves. Nevertheless it did provide that vital opening for Ulster Unionists to copper fasten their attachment to Great Britain and their separateness from the rest of Ireland. Within three days of the Paris meeting, Sir Basil Brooke was being briefed by Attlee at Chequers on the outcome.[62] Sir Basil had no objections to Éire leaving the Commonwealth; in fact it emphasized the differences between Northern Ireland and the rest of Ireland but he was most anxious to take advantage of that opportunity to strengthen the ties between Northern Ireland and Great Britain. He asked for a statutory guarantee that the status of Northern Ireland would not be altered without the consent of the Northern Irish parliament; he pressed for a seven year residence qualification in Northern Ireland in order to qualify for the franchise for the Northern Ireland parliament and a six months residence there in order to qualify for Westminster elections.[63] He was successful in most of his submissions.[64] If there

58 Lord Jowitt speaking in the House of Lords, 15 December 1948, Hansard, Columns 1092–1093. **59** Note of meeting with Mr Boland – present were Sir P. Liesching, Sir N. Brook, Archer and Pritchard, 7 January 1949, DO 103/104, PRO. **60** R.M. Heuston, 'British nationality and Irish citizenship', *International Affairs*, vol. 26, No. 1, January 1950, p. 87. **61** Sir Norman Brook to Attlee, 12 November 1948, DO 35/3964, PRO. **62** Downing Street press release, 22 November 1948, DO 35/3965, PRO. **63** N.E. Archer to Secretary of State for Commonwealth Relations, 25 November 1949, DO 35/3972, PRO. **64** He was granted his statutory guarantee; a five year residence for the

was any doubt before the repeal of the ERA about the survival of Northern Ireland as a separate entity, there were none afterwards. It was the tactics used rather than the repeal itself which brought that about.

By a strange irony only Sir Basil Brooke could have been completely satisfied with the repeal of the ERA. While MacBride had ditched the King, taken Ireland out of the Commonwealth and retained most of Ireland's erstwhile advantages, his vision of a United Ireland was severely dented. He would have been tempted to return to the Commonwealth had it guaranteed a united Ireland as would de Valera whose attachment to the ERA was based primarily on it providing a 'bridge' between the two sections of the island.[65] However, in both MacBride's and de Valera's estimations, it had outlived its usefulness by 1948, though it is doubtful if either of them realized that its repeal, far from leaving matters as they were before 1936, only further prejudiced the realization of their common goal. While Dr Evatt succeeded in retaining some link between Ireland and the Commonwealth countries and was most anxious that he be given credit for it, his ultimate aim of Ireland's reconciliation as a full member of the Commonwealth, was never achieved. Finally the outcome was most unpalatable for the British government; it had been forced on them; they considered that it was a dangerous precedent which left them open to charges of duplicity and possible retaliation by foreign countries. The Commonwealth itself had lost a member, albeit a recalcitrant one, but, as the Commonwealth Relations Office clearly recognized, that could be the beginning of the end. Within a short time the Commonwealth was to become so diffuse and amorphous that it was scarcely recognizable as such.

It is therefore quite clear that the Irish government did not anticipate Britain's initial response to its decision to repeal the ERA. This would suggest that either the Irish government had not thought through the full implications of its actions despite Costello's assertion that those actions had been long-standing government policy or on the other hand that the decision to repeal was an impulsive one. Ironically the latter interpretation is more flattering for the Irish as it provides some excuse for the short-sightedness of that policy decision. The Irish could not have anticipated Dr Evatt's intervention without

franchise for elections to the Northern Ireland parliament and a three month's residence for Westminster. 65 Meeting between Lord Rugby and de Valera on 16 October 1948 in which 'Dev said that opinion in Ireland had turned very heavily against the ERA – it had been his hope that this Act might prove to be a bridge – but it had done no good and had involved him and his government in difficulties and humiliation'. DO 35/3936, PRO. Later on 25 November 1948 de Valera told Rugby that 'he had hesitated about removing the ERA because it was intended to serve as a bridge to end partition – he could no longer hope for a solution along those lines.' DO 35/3963, PRO.

which Ireland would surely have suffered irreparable damage to its trade and restrictions on the movements of its citizens. By emphasizing the deliberate nature of their decision. Costello and MacBride are in fact acknowledging that a policy decision had been taken without regard to its consequences. Thus the impulsive response to the 'Roaring Meg' incident or the leak in the *Sunday Independent* may perhaps be less damaging.

8

Empire v. national interests in Australian-British relations during the 1930s

In a study of imperial economic relations between the wars, I.M. Drummond concluded that 'before anyone can reach finality, we must know more about the policy making process in each of the colonies and protectorates'.[1] While this article does not claim 'finality', the observations made are based on an examination of the decision-making process in one country, namely Australia. These conclusions confirm much of Drummond's thesis but they also tally with many of W.K. Hancock's earlier views on the subject. Drummond has chided Hancock for treating the 'problems of economic policy in the interwar Commonwealth as if the Commonwealth was an entity which could have an economic policy'.[2] The Commonwealth may not have had an economic policy as such, but the fact that some members at the time, especially Australia, firmly believed that it should have, is vital for an understanding of these countries' economic performances. In his 1936 study of Australian marketing, W.M. Smith recognised this fact and was highly critical of Australia's obsession with Empire preferences during the 1920s and 1930s.[3] With access to the public records in Canberra and London as well as to the private papers of many of the participants, it is possible to test the Hancock and Smith hypotheses and in the process to unravel the tangled web of national and imperial interests in Australian-British relations during the 1930s.

It is indeed ironic that prior to the 1930s Britain believed that it derived less economic advantage from the British Empire than her former colonies did. Throughout the 1920s the United Kingdom exported more to and imported more from foreign countries than it did from the Empire, though the margin was narrowing.[4] This may well account for its reluctance to have economic matters raised at imperial conferences; up till the 1930 Conference, the British government preferred to discuss constitutional, defence and cultural matters

1 I.M. Drummond, *Imperial economic policy, 1917–1939* (1974). 2 Ibid., p. 23; W.K. Hancock, *Survey of British Commonwealth Affairs* (1942), vol. 2, p. 427. 3 W.M. Smith, *The marketing of Australian and New Zealand primary produce* (1936). 4 Imperial Conference 1930, Secret Documents, Table 1, CP/290/10, Item 4, Australian Archives, Canberra (AA).

rather than economic integration. Being a free-trade country until 1932, Britain fought shy of proposals for imperial preference; these could have jeopardised its hold on world trade, while they could also prove electorally perilous as Baldwin found to his cost in 1923. Britain did not advance beyond the establishment of an Imperial Economic Committee in 1925 and an Empire Marketing Board in 1926. Both were quite innocuous bodies. As initially conceived in 1923, the Imperial Economic Committee was precluded from dealing with questions involving tariff policy and it was also obliged to obtain the consent of each interested Empire government before commencing any economic survey. Though later strengthened by Stanley Baldwin in 1925 to cater for the 'marketing within the United Kingdom of the food products of overseas parts of the Empire with a view to increasing the consumption of such products in the United Kingdom in preference to imports from foreign countries',[5] it was never more than a talking shop damned even before its foundation by E.H. Harding, a Dominion Office official, as a 'convenient waste paper basket for schemes of no particular interest'.[6] The Empire Marketing Board, though more flamboyant with its striking posters and its use of film for marketing purposes, still failed to increase the proportion of Empire products purchased in Britain. Until the devastation of the Depression, the United Kingdom appears to have been quite content with its share of Empire trade and it was not prepared to barter a share of its market for outlets elsewhere within the Empire. Economically, its relations with the Empire were selective, with British interests taking precedence over imperial. It was other considerations, however, which conditioned its concept of Empire and determined its loyalties.

With Australia it was otherwise. In a statement at the Imperial Conference in 1935, J.A. Lyons, Australian prime minister, made it abundantly clear that

> in the minds of those who first conceived and advocated preferential trade within the Empire, and those governments which in 1932, through their representatives, fashioned the Ottawa agreement, the object in view was *not* merely a material one bestowing benefits upon particular industries or interests in the United Kingdom or dominion – its immediate and particular intent was the quickening and growth of inter-Empire trade, but its higher aim was to make a substantial contribution to all that is embraced by the term British Empire, and all that

5 F.M. McDougall, 'The Imperial Economic Committee', p. 4, CP/103/12, Bundle 20, AA. 6 Harding to Llewellyn Smith, 17 July 1923, CO/352/262, Public Record Office, London (PRO).

> the Empire stands for as an influence in the civilisation today and tomorrow – any Empire reciprocal trading arrangement which does not progressively cultivate and make stronger the sentiment of Empire must fail [. . .] it is of equal importance that no foreign interest should be allowed to frustrate the high purpose of Ottawa.[7]

Material well-being and a crusade for moral regeneration via the British Empire were combined in this way. Though Lyons made his statement for public consumption, in private the Australians were far more concerned with the material rewards which they believed were inextricably bound up with the Empire, especially their relations with the mother country. There is no reason why they should not have espoused the non-material values or have found in the Empire a useful vehicle for that purpose, but nevertheless, assertions of these cultural loyalties provided a welcome gloss which diverted attention from more selfish and less altruistic reasons for their commitment to the British Empire. Lyons himself was near panic during the closing days of the Ottawa Conference, when in the isolation of his office in the wilds of Canberra, he convinced himself and the few left around him that Australian pastoral interests were in danger. He immediately telegraphed a series of instructions to Bruce that could well have jeopardised the very foundation of the Empire itself, had Bruce taken them seriously or had the British taken fright at the extremes of these trading demands.[8]

The genesis of Australian imperial sentiment and its manifestation in the 1920s and 1930s can be traced to a remarkable and unlikely Australian official in London, F.L. McDougall. From his arrival in London in 1922, as a member of a fruit-growers' mission in search of a larger share of the British market, McDougall was indefatigable in his efforts to promote Empire trade by means of reciprocal preferences. He was to remain in London, encouraged by Bruce, long after the mission had returned to Australia and in an unofficial

7 Appendix to Economic Discussions between the United Kingdom and Australian Ministers, 4 April 1935, CP/290/10, AA. 8 Lyons to Bruce, 19 August 1932, CP/103/12, Bundle 2, AA, where he indicated that 'we consider proposal to raise meat prices in England by restriction upon dominion meat as well as on foreign will have greater disorganising effect on Australia export than upon that of other dominions', and he advised that 'on no account make any further substantial concession without consulting us'. On the matter of the later Article X of the Ottawa Agreement, Lyons cabled Bruce 'We consider the words "on the basis of the relative cost of economical and efficient production" are almost meaningless and unless altered to more definitive phraseology very likely serious misunderstanding by all interests'. Had Bruce followed Lyons' advice it is doubtful if Australia would have reached an agreement at Ottawa. F.L. McDougall to his brother Norman, 26 September 1923, McDougall papers, National Library of Australia (NLA). See also W.J. Hudson and W. Way (eds), *Letters from a 'Secret Service Agent'* (Canberra 1986).

capacity he was to storm government and opposition alike in his quest for Empire preferential trade – he was indeed the first great Australian lobbyist. His status was never defined; he was in Australia House, London, but was never of it; he accepted obscurity lest he upset the Civil Service establishment.[9] 'Your little brother', he wrote to his brother back in Renmark, 'was posing as an expert on subjects in which he knew nothing';[10] and when he asked Bruce exactly what his position was, Bruce told him that in his 'more uplifted moments he could call himself the confidential representative of the Australian Prime Minister – when less influential, a secret service agent!'[11] This was the man who did more than anyone else during the 1920s to convert British politicians of all parties to the merits of tariffs as means of augmenting Empire trade; it was McDougall who also did most of the preparatory work in London prior to the Ottawa Conference and who earned the admiration not only of officials in London but also of those in Canberra who might have resented his interference. He was privy to policy making at the highest level in Australia – writing to him in January 1932, Bruce said that 'he would be kept fully informed of anything that is being done here and that all information you send here will receive fullest consideration'.[12] Throughout the 1930s he was economic adviser at Australia House and played a valuable role in all trade matters. It was indeed a remarkable achievement for one who deprecatingly referred to himself as 'a working farmer, with no knowledge of economics, politics, or anything'.[13]

What was the secret of his success? While there is no denying his undoubted ability and energy and his brilliance as a communicator, these talents could well have been wasted had it not been for a fortuitous meeting in 1922 with the future Australian Prime Minister, Stanley Melbourne Bruce.[14] From that meeting, there developed a remarkable relationship between the two men – the reserved Bruce seems to have enjoyed an empathy with McDougall that he failed to establish with most others save, perhaps Sir Henry Gullett or Sir Antony Eden. At the time of McDougall's death, Bruce is reported to have said, 'I never really knew whether Bruce made McDougall or McDougall made Bruce, whichever it was, it was a damned fine combination,' and on another occasion he remarked that 'McDougall brings me a new idea every

9 F.L. McDougall to his brother Norman, 26 September 1923, McDougall Papers, National Library of Australia (NLA). See also Hudson and Way (eds), *Letters from a 'Secret Service Agent'*. **10** Ibid., 5 September 1923. **11** Ibid., 2 February 1924. **12** Bruce to McDougall, 27 January 1932, CP/103/12, Bundle 21, AA. F.L. McDougall to his brother Norman, 19 August 1923, McDougall Papers, NLA. **13** F.L. McDougall to his brother Norman, 19 August 1923, McDougall papers, NLA. **14** Ibid., 10 November 1922.

morning'.[15] McDougall recognised that and in fact wrote to his brother, 'You see I have a very considerable pull with Bruce',[16] and on another occasion he mentioned that he had played his 'first round of golf with Bruce'.[17] When Bruce visited London as Prime Minister in October 1923, McDougall could write to his brother that he had 'sat at the Conference listening to Mr Bruce's speech – which was naturally of great interest to me because I had worked up the whole speech with him'.[18] It was this leverage that McDougall put to such effect in the cause of Empire preferential trade. Because of the strategic positions held by Bruce, first as Prime Minister, then as chief Australian negotiator at Ottawa and later as High Commissioner in London, he was able to exercise considerable influence in that cause and it was this that McDougall exploited to the full. While it is doubtful whether Bruce needed convincing, McDougall's constant barrage of ideas and plans ensured that Bruce did not grow tepid.

McDougall's vision of Empire has been neatly described by Wendy Way as one 'capable of self-sufficiency, able through mutual cooperation to develop its vast resources and solve all its problems', a feature that had been so convincingly demonstrated during World War 1.[19] This found favour with the Bruce-Page Government in the 1920s, which had as an essential anchor of its policies the interdependence of members of the British Empire; with countries like Australia disposing of their agricultural surpluses in Britain and the latter finding markets for their industrial goods in the Commonwealth.[20] In his pre-Ottawa deliberations, Bruce wrote to McDougall that they 'should strive to arrive at a basis which will enable the British government to afford an equality of treatment in the British Market to the whole Empire'.[21] Even when it entailed a retreat from Australia's long insistence on a duty on mutton and lamb at Ottawa, Bruce was prepared on the final day of the Ottawa Conference to give way, even against the explicit instructions of Lyons, lest 'we would imperil the possibility of the Conference being a success with disastrous results to the British Empire and probably the whole world'.[22] 'I regard Ottawa', he wrote, 'as only the start in laying the foundation. The work will have to go for-

15 W. Way, 'Bruce's Secret Service Agent, F.L. McDougall in London 1923–26', unpublished paper delivered to the Department of International Relations, Research School of Pacific Studies, Australian National University, 24 May 1984, p. 22. **16** F.L. McDougall to his brother Norman, 20 December 1923, McDougall papers., NLA **17** Ibid., 9 September 1924. **18** Ibid., 11 October 1923. **19** W. Way, 'Bruce's Secret Service Agent, F.L. McDougall in London 1923–26', p. 5. **20** W.H. Richmond, 'S.M. Bruce and Australian Economic Policy, 1923–29', *Australian Economic History Review*, vol. 22, 1983, pp. 238–57. **21** Bruce to McDougall, 3 March 1932, CP/103/12/, Bundle 21, AA. **22** Bruce to Lyons, 23 August 1932, J.A. Lyons Papers, NLA.

ward for a long time after the Ottawa Conference has been held.' But he was not without hope, especially as he had accepted a posting in London which he expected would ensure that 'this continuous work' was kept alive.[23]

This was a well-contrived plan and one that Bruce adhered to in the 1930s. As Honorary Minister assisting the Treasurer in Lyons' Cabinet in 1932,[24] he was responsible for the preparation and the execution of government policy at Ottawa; as Resident Minister and later as High Commissioner in London, he not only saw to the implementation of those policies, but in a remarkable way he played a major role in their formulation. Being an ex-Prime Minister undoubtedly helped, but Sir George Reid and Andrew Fisher had also held that office and there is no evidence to suggest that it enhanced their standing in London or allowed them to play an important role in the formulation of Australian policy. Bruce's real strength and the main reason for his effectiveness in London was the fact that he retained the confidence and the respect of former parliamentary colleagues still in influential positions in Canberra. In certain respects he was the link, albeit 12,000 miles distant, which held the Coalition together after Earl Page's Country Party decided to join with Lyons' United Australia Party (UAP) in 1934. Bruce and Page had worked closely in office during the 1920s and such was the latter's regard for Bruce that he pleaded with him in November 1933 to re-enter Australian politics. 'I felt', he wrote to Bruce

> and many hundreds and thousands also felt that just now Australia was peculiarly your place, that you could bring a unifying influence and a long experience into operation, that no other man could. With that in mind, I tried to keep Flinders open for you but without success and I suppose it would have been useless anyhow.[25]

It was Bruce's promise of success in London that helped preserve and maintain the uneasy balance between the high-tariff UAP and the low-tariff Country Party; Australia's agricultural goods could be sold in England while the tariff clauses of the Ottawa Agreement would protect Australian industry. And on Lyons' sudden death in April 1939, it was to Bruce that Page looked for national leadership.

23 Bruce to McDougall, 3 March 1932, CP/103/12, Bundle 21, AA. **24** Lyons Papers, Box 1, Folder 9, NLA, being the correspondence between Lyons and Bruce concerning the composition of his Cabinet; Lyons offered Bruce the post of Honorary Minister to assist the Treasury and Bruce, while accepting it, pointed out that 'a better impression would be created' in London, if he were appointed 'Vice President of the Executive Council'. **25** Page to Bruce, 28 November 1933, CP/23M/104, Item 2, AA.

Bruce enjoyed an equally close relationship with Sir Henry Gullett, Minister for Trade Treaties between 1934 and 1937. Gullett had been Bruce's assistant at Ottawa. So impressed was Bruce with Gullett that he wrote to Lyons in October 1932 telling him 'how extraordinary well Gullett has done here', especially the way 'in which he got on with the British Ministers and British officials', and he even recommended him 'as a future Resident Minister in London'.[26] When Gullett was appointed Minister for Trade Treaties in 1934, Bruce was overjoyed; he now had a close confidant in a most strategic position. 'It is essential', Bruce wrote to Gullett, 'that we should work together and there should be complete understanding between us if you are to succeed in your job, which I regard as of supreme importance at present time'.[27] He need not have worried. Gullett was in total agreement with Bruce, 'even if we are at variance with a good deal of expressed government policy',[28] and Bruce looked forward very much to having Gullett and his wife Penelope stay with him in London in 1935.[29]

While Bruce's relations with Lyons may have been a little frayed during the hectic last days of the Ottawa Conference, Lyons never doubted Bruce's perspicacity: 'We make these suggestions, but leave matter to your judgement.'[30] And when the outcome was at variance with Lyons' instructions, far from reprimanding Bruce, he telegraphed his congratulations: 'We are all delighted with the news.'[31] He subsequently wrote expressing his appreciation of the 'splendid fight you and Gullett put up on behalf of Australia'.[32] After that, Bruce had only to maintain the pressure, which he did through his correspondence, his annual reports and his personal contact with Lyons when the latter visited London in 1935 and 1937, to ensure that the Australian government would not waver in its espousal of empire preferential trade.[33] On the occasion of the 1937 general election, Bruce was even presumptuous enough to submit proposals for the government's platform, the main one being that 'the government's policy of cooperation with Great Britain as opposed to the opposition's policy of isolation was the only practical method of ensuring Australia's safety', and he pointed to the experience of the Irish Free State as a salutary lesson to those who might be tempted to think otherwise.[34]

26 Bruce to Lyons, 23 August 1932, Lyons Papers, NLA. **27** Bruce to Gullett, 12 October 1934, CP/23M/104, Item 2, AA. **28** Gullet to Bruce, 29 October 1934, CP/23M/104, Item 2, AA. **29** Bruce to Gullett, 13 December 1934, CP/23M/104, Item 2, AA. **30** Lyons to Bruce, 19 August 1932, CP/103/12, Bundle 2, AA. **31** Lyons to Bruce, 22 August 1932, CP/103/12, Bundle 20, AA. **32** Lyons to Bruce, 2 November 1932, Lyons Papers, NLA. **33** See, for example, 'High Commissioners' Annual Reports', CRS A601, Items 130/30/1; 130/30/2; 133/30/3, AA. **34** Bruce to Lyons, 7 July 1937, CP/23M/104, AA. 'Broadly my idea is that in the opening stages you should say enough: 1. to make clear the seriousness of the international situation; 2. that the Government's pol-

During the 1930s, Bruce and McDougall had all the semblances of a government in exile – the only difference being that they were far more effective because of their standing with the government in Australia. While undoubtedly they could tap a residue of good-will towards the Empire in Australia, they cemented that attachment by demonstrating that Australia's own interests were synonymous with success in London. The tragedy was that they were less successful in London itself and, except for the immediate pre-Ottawa years, they encountered strong opposition there in their imperial crusade. The former colony had more of the traditional Empire spirit than the metropolitan centre itself.

The Ottawa Agreement, far from being the climax of established British policy, was in fact an aberration arising from immediate circumstances of the world-wide depression. McDougall might welcome the Imperial Economic Committee and the Empire Marketing Board as breaches in the prevailing economic orthodoxy, but he exaggerated their significance; they merely tinkered with the system, barely scratching the surface of entrenched laissez-faire attitudes.[35] Bruce recognised this at Ottawa when he acknowledged that up to that point 'on the economic side, progress had been slight', and he accepted that this aspect of the 1930 Imperial Conference 'was a failure'. However he also pointed out:

> since 1930 we have been faced by a radically changed position. Then the world depression was serious, but in the last two years it has deepened and widened until now it is of the gravest intensity.[36]

Being a response to an immediate situation, the new arrangement was unlikely to prove permanent, especially if it were felt that the reaction was precipitate and the outcome less favourable than anticipated. Still, it did mean that for the first and only time during the inter-war years, British self-interest was not confined to the cultural or the defence aspects of Empire but extended to imperial economic development.

The Ottawa Agreement was a great triumph for Australia. With the exception of disappointments in the case of meat, Australia achieved all that it

icy of cooperation with Great Britain as opposed to the opposition's policy of isolationism is the only practical method of ensuring Australia's safety; 3. that the Government has a sound and practical defence policy as opposed to the opposition's extremely unsound and impracticable one. Give the story of cuts in interest rates, including the history of the conversions in London, bring out the point that while the cuts in social services, salaries and wages have been restored, the reduction in interest rates and government securities has been maintained etc.' 35 McDougall to Bruce, 4 February 1932, CP/103/12, Bundle 21, AA. 36 Statement by Bruce at Ottawa, 22 July 1932, CP/103/12, Bundle 21, AA.

desired – free entry for most of its goods to Britain with nearly all of them enjoying a preferential tariff over foreigners. The only reciprocity conceded was a level of preference for British goods in Australia to be determined by the Tariff Board but open (according to the Australian understanding of the Ottawa Agreement) to modification by the Australian Parliament. In practice, Australia got almost everything it requested in return for very few concessions. The success at Ottawa was a tribute mainly to McDougall, Bruce and Gullett, with the decisive breakthrough being apparently made early on by McDougall. In a letter to Bruce on 10 February 1932, McDougall wrote that he

> was delighted that the Cabinet finally decided to make the preferences available pending the Ottawa discussions – up to February 3, the government's intention was to have extended the preferences immediately to the colonies, but to reserve the dominion's preferences until after Ottawa. I do not know what influence my representation had but Malcolm MacDonald evidently thinks that his interview with Neville Chamberlain after our talk had a determining effect.[37]

This was indeed a vital breakthrough because it meant that Britain had shown its hand even before the negotiations had started. The Import Duties Act of February 1932 imposed a 10% ad valorem duty on all imports but suspended it in the case of the dominions until 15 November, pending the outcome of the Ottawa Conference. Britain had made its concessions without ascertaining the dominions' response. It was later to regret this declaration of its hand. At its meeting with McDougall on 7 April 1932, J.H. Thomas, Secretary of State for the Dominions, 'started the conversation by making clear how impressed he was with the difficulties likely to attend the Ottawa Conference. By its actions over the Import Duties Act, the government here had thrown all its cards on the table.' In a somewhat belated attempt to redress the situation, Thomas 'was bound to say that the response which this gesture had elicited had not been so good as he would have liked, and he asked Mr McDougall to bear in mind that November 15, 1932 was a very relevant date'.[38]

The British had left themselves little scope for bargaining and the Australian negotiators were quick to exploit that deficiency. With the exception of their willingness to withdraw demands for a tariff on foreign mutton and lamb and accept quotas instead, the Australians made no concessions at Ottawa.

37 McDougall to Bruce, 10 February 1932, CP/103/12, Bundle 21, AA. 38 E.J. Harding's account of meeting between J.H. Thomas and F.L. McDougall, 7 April 1932, Dominion Office 35 (DO 35), 240/8831H/35, PRO.

Bruce made it clear that he 'would not be prepared, even for the purpose of saving the Conference, to acquiesce in any arrangement with regard to meat that did not give a sure and certain benefit to Australia',[39] Sir Geoffrey Whiskard, the Dominion Office Official present at Ottawa, was furious; he felt that 'none of our masters has the backbone of a louse'. In fact he observed that 'the extent to which the Dominions are prepared to ask for everything and concede nothing has been an eye opener for Hailsham, Neville Cunliffe-Lister and Gilmour'.[40] He quoted Neville Chamberlain as saying that 'he had put up at Ottawa with insults from Bennett and Bruce such as he would never had imagined it possible he should have borne'.[41] Whiskard also observed that the British Ministers were 'afraid' of Bennett and Bruce so that when they 'demanded further concessions – brutally as if they were dictating terms to a beaten enemy, as indeed they were – all were at once conceded'.[42] This success was not lost on the rest of the British civil service in London. Sir Henry Fountain of the Board of Trade was spurred to write to Whiskard in September 1932 when the matter of further concessions in respect of pig meat arose, advising him 'not to give way too readily to the wish of the Australians to continue screwing concessions out of us up till the last possible moment.' 'They pursued this policy at Ottawa, but now that the agreements are signed we ought to be free of their importunities.'[43] Even as late as October – two months after the conclusion of the Conference – British civil servants were still licking their wounds. In a letter, again to Whiskard, Twentyman of the Treasury, advised that 'We understand that he [Bruce] has been going about saying that the United Kingdom officials do not know how to bargain and that it is not his job to teach them, and that if they had been more alert they could have got more concessions from his government.'[44]

Is it any wonder, then, that Gullett should have bragged in the *Sydney Morning Herald* that the Ottawa Agreement 'conferred more benefits upon the Australian farmers and graziers and pastoralists than fell to any other single dominion', or that the Board of Trade should six years later note that there was 'more widespread dissatisfaction in this country with regard to the agreement with Australia than in regard to any other of the Ottawa Agreements'?[45] These were two sides of the same coin, the British believing that their expectations of the Conference had been frustrated by the Australians, whose naked opportunism soured recent expressions of imperial economic altruism. The

39 Bruce to Lyons, 23 August 1932, Lyons papers, NLA. **40** Whiskard to Harding, 16 August 1932, DO 35, 121/6, PRO. **41** Ibid., 19 August 1932. **42** Ibid., 22 August 1932. **43** Fountain to Whiskard, 20 September 1932, DO 35, 273/9261/7, PRO. **44** Twentyman to Whiskard, 12 October 1932, DO 35, 273/9261/11, PRO.

Australians, of course, did not see it that way. In his report to the House of Representatives on the Ottawa Agreement, Lyons emphasised that the undertakings at Ottawa

> practically coincided with the tariff policy which he had announced in his policy speech before the Federal Election last year [. . .] it was very gratifying that the policy then announced should have so completely met the needs of the time and that it had become the basis of the great Inter Empire Agreement reached at Ottawa.[46]

This was to defend the British Empire in Australian terms! In Australian eyes, there was total harmony between Australia's own economic interests and those of the British Empire. The agreement might have been made on Australian terms, but these could still be rationalised in terms of Empire altruism. But the British were not deceived, Ottawa left Britain with a sense of resentment and a determination that it should not happen again. Empire considerations would not in the future impede national interests, even if that meant accommodating foreigners. The conjunction of interests at Ottawa was to prove ephemeral while the triad of mother country, dominion and empire was to reassert itself, with all the ambiguities inherent in that combination.

The kernel of the problem for Australia during the 1930s was that it had been too successful at Ottawa. That success bred a complacency that was not justified, while it heightened expectations that were unattainable. The Empire had paid dividends at Ottawa and Australian officials both in London and in Canberra were firmly convinced that it would continue to do so. As a result, they were blinded to opportunities elsewhere and formulated policies on the assumption that they could continue to extract further concessions from the British. Both of these attitudes proved disastrous; they deflected Australia's attention from valuable markets elsewhere, especially in Japan, while they reinforced perceptions of Britain that were based on false hypotheses. The Australians failed to recognise that in the 1930s the British Empire meant something quite different to Britain from what it meant to them. At Ottawa British and Australian views had coincided because their interests were identical, but subsequently these diverged and Australia refused to recognise the fact. Accordingly, its picture of Britain and Britain's trading role within the Empire was distorted for most of the 1930s, with calamitous results for Aus-

45 *Sydney Morning Herald*, 24 September 1932; Board of Trade Memo, 28 April 1938, DO 35, 749/01/46, PRO. 46 W.C. Hankinson to Under-Secretary Dominion Office, 3 September 1932, reporting Lyons' speech, DO 35, 1 273/9261/13, PRO.

tralian trade negotiations. The remarkable feature, however, was that in spite of failure or minimal gain, Australia did not swerve from its committed path – surely ample testimony to the exaggerated expectations created by the Ottawa bonanza. The Dominion Office did little to dampen these aspirations; on the contrary, it tended to confirm them.

The Dominion Office was Australia's friend at Whitehall, but Australia never appreciated that the Dominion Office carried little weight in the Cabinet or that its Secretary of State was low in the official hierarchy.[47] The Dominion Office's benevolence was seldom matched by tangible results but the atmosphere was congenial. Bruce in particular enjoyed an empathy with Dominion Office officials that seemed at times to compensate for the lack of progress in trade negotiations. They shared a common concept of Empire, N.E. Archer, a Dominion Office official, argued that more than just the trading needs of the United Kingdom were at stake in imperial relations. The British government should pay 'much regard to wider considerations',[48] a clear echo of Lyons' speech to the 1935 Imperial Conference. Small wonder that Bruce was impressed and, through him, his parliamentary colleagues in Australia were impressed also. If the Lyons government needed further encouragement they had in Canberra from 1936 onwards a British High Commissioner, Sir Geoffrey Whiskard, who was himself a former Dominion Office official.

The diet served in London and Canberra was therefore readily digested by the Australians. They could hardly have chosen the ingredients better themselves as it seemed to meet their needs in every respect. The only problem was that it did not represent British government thinking. In trading matters it was the Board of Trade and not the Dominion Office that wrote the menu in those years and neither Bruce nor the Australian government found much sympathy in that quarter, as the following 1936 Board of Trade memo makes clear:

> In 1932, the value of foreign trade fell still further to £200,000,000. In spite of pressure the United Kingdom refused to make trade agreements with any foreign country until agreement had been made first with the Dominions in Ottawa. The United Kingdom as part of an Empire policy imposed duties and restrictions on a large proportion of imports from foreign producing countries [. . .] she went as far as it was possible to go in this direction without unduly endangering her export

47 Garner J, *The Commonwealth Office* (1978), pp. 26, 137, et al. 48 Note on United Kingdom-Australian Trade negotiations prepared by N.E. Archer, DO 35,750/01/74, PRO.

> trade. As a result Australia enjoys in the United Kingdom substantial tariff preferences [. . .] After Ottawa, the United Kingdom had to consider how she could secure and if possible recover badly diminished trade with foreign countries and to this end, she embarked upon negotiations of a number of trade agreements. In almost every case, the foreign countries concerned pressed for the revision or modification of the Ottawa duties and restrictions which affected their trade. This pressure was resisted. Considerable difficulty was experienced in reaching agreements which would have real value for the United Kingdom exporting industries. And it proved necessary to accord foreign countries concessions which involved either immediate sacrifice on the part of the United Kingdom or a limitation on the protection which could be afforded those interests in the future.[49]

The Board of Trade could be quite curt in implementing these policies, as will be apparent from its handling of the Trade Diversion episode in 1936 and by its participation in the 1938 renegotiation of the Ottawa Agreement. And there was little the Dominion Office could do to redress the balance; bland expressions of Empire good-will were no substitute for trading successes.

Accordingly, relations between the Dominion Office and the Board of Trade were often strained when the subject of Dominion trade, especially Australian trade, was at issue. This was apparent both in Britain and in Australia. The Board of Trade was outraged when the Dominion Office provided a brief that was sympathetic to Australian industry for Lord De La Warr, the Lord Privy Seal, when he visited Australia in 1938. De La Warr later warned the Dominion Office against the 'anti-Australian bias' in the Board of Trade.[50] In Australia, relations between both departments' representatives were equally strained. In 1936, E.J. Harding, permanent Under-Secretary in the Dominion Office, took the unusual step of cautioning his old colleague, Whiskard, about his relations with R.W. Dalton, the Senior Trade Commissioner in Australia. Harding advised Whiskard that he should consult with Dalton as the latter 'had a profound knowledge of the requirements of Australia'.[51]

He was right. In trading matters, Dalton was far superior to Whiskard: he had a detailed grasp of most items of manufacture in Australia, as well as hav-

49 Board of Trade memo, 22 May 1936, Page papers, NLA. 50 De La Warr to Secretary of State Dominion Affairs, 3 May 1938, DO 35, 749/01/46, PRO. 51 Harding to Whiskard, 8 July 1936, DO 35, 278/9279/156, PRO.

ing a comprehensive view of the agricultural situation. He had been the main British negotiator during the pre-Ottawa discussions and since then he had produced extensive reports for the Board of Trade on most Australian industries.

Whiskard, however, ignored the advice given by Harding and so, with the exception of the Dominion Office, Australia had few allies in Whitehall.[52] All other ministries shared, in one way or another, in the resentment after Ottawa; many, however, had their own peculiar grievances. Walter Elliott, Secretary of State for Agriculture from 1932 to 1936, and W.S. Morrison, who succeeded him in that office from 1936 to 1939, found that as British agriculture became more intensive during the 1930s, it was hampered by the terms of the Ottawa Agreement. These ministers argued that the Dominions were only entitled to an expanding share of meat imports, at the expense of foreigners but not at the expense of the British producer. The President of the Board of Trade argued hotly that Australia was reneging on its Ottawa commitments. He accused the Australian Tariff Board of misinterpreting Article X of that Treaty and he was also furious on those few occasions when the Australian government refused to impose a whip when Tariff Board reports were presented to Parliament and rejected on a free vote. The Lord Chancellor was horrified at the request of the Tasmanian government for a voice in the selection of Judicial Lords in the James Case in 1936, the major Australian trading and market issue to reach the Privy Council in the 1930s. The Lord Chancellor's view of Empire conformed to the usual British specification, Britain first, the Empire second, and the Dominions last.[53] Accordingly, the Australians found themselves out on a limb. They had exaggerated their standing with the British government and the number of their friends at court, and later they refused to recognise that reality even in the face of repeated rebuffs.

A possible explanation of this apparent political masochism is the complex role played by Bruce in the entire process. He was largely responsible, through his activities in London and his contacts in Canberra, for formulating an Empire policy that was essentially sterile from 1933 onwards because of the shift in British imperial perceptions. He was also present and actively involved in London when Australia took steps to implement these policies and invariably, when these failed, Bruce was also at hand to mount a rescue operation – he was both arsonist and fire-fighter. His greatest gift was that people believed him, especially in Australia. He could point to bland imperial sentiments as

52 For further particulars on this exchange see details on Harding/Dalton/Whiskard relationship on pp 77–8 above. 53 25 May 1936, DO 35, 390/10892/16, PRO.

major achievements, to niggardly concessions as major breakthroughs, to failures as successes and to other people's successes as his own. It was indeed a remarkable performance for a High Commissioner.

This was the case in most areas of financial and trading negotiations between Britain and Australia in the 1930s. Cain and Glynn have shown quite convincingly in their examination of the British-Australian debt conversion of 1933, that, far from dictating terms, Australia, and in particular Bruce, had to bow to Britain's requirements in both the timing and the extent of the conversions. Bruce might well have told 250 members of the Melbourne Chamber of Commerce in 1939 that he 'was able to convert £200,000,000 of Australia's overseas loan by "scaring hell" out of the Chancellor of the Exchequer and the Governor of the Bank of England', but Cain and Glynn provide evidence to show that he did nothing of the kind. They conclude that 'unflustered by claims of dire political exigency in the Antipodes, the British pursued their objective with firmness and resource, making relatively minor concessions as occasion required. Altogether, the game played seems to have been one of Britain's choosing.'[54]

The same could be said of the interminable meat negotiations which absorbed so much time during the 1930s and which yielded so little. Suffice to say that the return was minimal, a mere gain of 5% spread over three years from 1935. Page argued in 1936 that British purchases from foreign countries were excessive: in 1935 she still bought 208,600 tons of foreign butter from foreign countries out of a total import of 480,000 tons. She derived 486,500 tons of beef from foreign sources out of a total import of 625,600 tons. She bought 14,986,000 great hundreds of eggs from foreign suppliers out of 19,798,000 great hundreds.[55]

But Bruce cautioned Gullett about the hazards of these European markets: 'the more I see of Central European countries, the more convinced I am of their complete unreliability and disreputable instincts'.[56] Accordingly, he recommended that they should cultivate the British market; in a similar vein he wrote to Lyons advising the government 'to recognise the importance of the British market to Australia'.[57] Lyons recognised the possibility of alternative markets but was reluctant to fully exploit them. At the Launceston Agricultural Show in 1936, he said: 'We want to trade with Japan but such trade must

54 N. Cain and S. Glynn, 'Imperial relations under Strain: the British-Australian debt contretemps of 1933', *Australian Economic History Review*, vol. 25, 1985, pp. 39–58. 55 Page papers (undated) NLA. 56 Bruce to Gullett, 13 December 1934, CP/23M/104, Item 2, AA. 57 Bruce to Lyons, 19 December 1934, Lyons papers, NLA.

be on a basis that does not involve embarrassment with other good customer countries, particularly the United Kingdom'.[58] Thus while Britain was moving further afield in its quest for alternative markets, Australia was becoming more and more introspective. This was nowhere more apparent that in the disastrous trade diversion scheme of 1936.

In that instance, Australia was misled into diverting trade from Japan and the United States to Great Britain, on the assumption that Britain shared Australia's view of Empire and would reciprocate. Accordingly, the Australian government did not square the deal with Great Britain beforehand, believing that to be unnecessary. But the British did not respond. Even McDougall was forced to concede that 'Australia had acted prematurely [. . .] and that it would have been better if she had held her hand until the conclusion of the meat negotiations'.[59] But it was not only in respect of meat that Australia failed to win concessions from the British; she also failed to obtain from Britain a public acknowledgement of the benefits which Britain derived from Australia. The President of the Board of Trade refused to make that acknowledgement because the 'Commonwealth government had thought it best to reach their decision without prior consultation with the United Kingdom' and also because a public endorsement like that might prove embarrassing for the United Kingdom's relations with the United States, Canada and Japan.[60] Earle Page, Australian Minister for Commerce, pleaded with the British 'to say something that would support them in their gesture to assist the United Kingdom trade' in view of the 'extraordinary steps with regard to cotton and rayon duties' which they were taking, but Walter Runciman, the President of the Board of Trade, would not budge. He said that 'the United Kingdom government was very satisfied for the action proposed to be taken in regard to Japanese competition, but this action could not be regarded as being agreed between the two governments'.[61]

Britain was not prepared to jeopardise its foreign prospects. Australia had no hesitation and suffered accordingly. In 1936 Japan was Australia's second largest customer for wool and that trade was growing. For the six months to June 1936, the main wool-buying season, Japan took 25% of Australian wool as against 17% for the corresponding period in the previous years; during the same period, Britain's share of purchases fell from 43% to 36%.[62] Because of the diversionary episode, Australian wool exports to Japan fell from approximately 172,000,000 kins in 1935 to 59,000,000 kins in 1938 or from 94% of

58 Speech, 19 September 1936, Box 2, Folder 15, Lyons papers, NLA. **59** DO 35, 278/9279/141, PRO. **60** DO 35, 278/9279/119, PRO. **61** Ibid. **62** *The Sun*, 25 January 1937.

Japanese wool imports to 67% and for the first time Australia incurred a deficit in her trade balance with Japan.[63] It was little wonder that Earle Page should have been 'apparently struck dumb' when Britain refused to make any concessions whatsoever on meat at his meeting with British Ministers in London in June 1936.[64] In fact he was tempted to abandon discussions and had it not been for the timely intervention of Bruce, the Australian delegation could well have returned home empty-handed. As already mentioned, Bruce succeeded in extracting a concession of a 5% increase in meat exports over three years at the expense of foreign countries, especially Argentina – small recompense, however, for the loss of the Japanese wool market. It is doubtful if Australia would have found itself in that predicament had it not been for the heightened expectations generated by Bruce in the first instance.

The final episode in this Empire saga, of even more tragic proportions than the previous one, was the abysmal attempt by the Australians in 1938 to renegotiate the Ottawa Agreement in its favour. The renegotiations reflected more than anything else Australia's erroneous view of Britain's economic rule within the Empire during the 1930s and as such they were the culmination of the unrealistic atmosphere engendered in London and in Canberra by the preferential Empire brigade. No less than three senior Cabinet Ministers and nine officials were away from Australia for four and a half months at a cost to the Australian Exchequer of £15,466.[65] The mission was an unmitigated failure, though like many previous trade negotiations during the 1930s it was nevertheless sold to a gullible Australian public as a national triumph.

The instructions which the Australian Cabinet drew up for the delegation included the following:

> Articles 8, 9, 10, 11, 12, 13, 14 and 15 are to be deleted from the Ottawa Agreement; Australian products are to be free of duty and free from quantitative limitation in the British market and the United Kingdom is to be encouraged to promote Australian interest in the European market.

63 Okorasho, Nippon Gaikoku Boeki Nempyo 1936–1939, quoted in T. Fukushima, *The Australian-Japanese trade dispute, 1936*, Department of International Relations, University of Tokyo September 1981. 64 Machtig to Whiskard, 30 June 1936, DO35, 258/9105/3/99, PRO London. See also telephone call between Page and Lyons, 24 June 1936, in which Page said 'What has been offered to Australia was useless, and he told the British representatives that we could not possibly accept it as an Empire policy: it was going back on the principles of Ottawa.' Lyons papers, Box. 5, NLA. 65 R.G. Menzies to F.M. Forde, 19 May 1939, House of Representatives, Canberra.

The only concession which the delegation could make would be 'some modifications of preferences at present enjoyed by Australia if it can be seen that any such modifications may lead to an expansion of international trade'.[66] This was hardly a vital negotiating counter since, with the exception of sugar, wine, spirits and tobacco, upon which duties were imposed for revenue purposes, all Australian goods were admitted to the United Kingdom free of duty and so did not require preferences. On 4 April 1938, these proposals were dispatched to London.

The Board of Trade's initial reaction was one of amazement – semi-officially they described the proposals as 'fantastic'.[67] The Board of Trade could point to the rise of £26,000,000 in the value of Australian exports to the United Kingdom between 1931 and 1937 and also to the fact that in each year during the 1930s, Australia had a substantial surplus in its balance of trade with the United Kingdom. Further, the Board of Trade argued that 'with the exception of wheat and wool, the Australian primary industries were particularly dependent upon the United Kingdom market for the disposal of her export surplus'. In terms of Australia's total export, the United Kingdom had furnished a market for 44.9% of the total exports from Australia during the year ending 30 June 1931; in 1936–37 the percentage was 49.9. While the Commonwealth government could point to a considerable volume of reductions of protective duties and comparatively few increases, the Board of Trade replied:

> the protective tariff wall was so absurdly high at the time of Ottawa that there was much scope for reduction without seriously impairing the position of the local manufacturer. A large number of the reduced duties were at levels of 20% to 30% ad valorem and when exchange and primary duties were taken into consideration, it was probably safe to say that in these cases the reduced duties were still too high to give a material improvement in the United Kingdom position.

This was particularly galling for the Board of Trade because the functioning of the Australian Tariff Board along agreed principles as codified in Articles 9 to 12 of the Ottawa Agreement had been demanded as a quid pro quo for the free entry of Australian goods into the United Kingdom. Thus:

> while Australia had entered into the immediate enjoyment of all the benefits which we accorded to her goods under the Ottawa Agreement,

66 Trade Negotiations 1938, General Instructions to the Delegates proceeding Overseas, p. 2, 1667/430/ B/65, AA. **67** DO 35, 749/01/40, PRO.

> we on the other hand had to be content, in the main, with various conditional undertakings in regard to the future treatment of United Kingdom goods imported into Australia [. . .] The degree to which those promises would be kept would depend entirely upon the political exigencies of the time and not upon the merits of the particular concessions which may be sought.

The Board of Trade concluded that 'if the articles were amended to suit the Australian manufacturers they would be practically worthless to us'.[68]

They were not amended. On all points, the Australians failed to make any progress whatever. In effect, they had little to offer the British and mere invocations of Empire solidarity cut little ice with the Board of Trade negotiators, especially Oliver Stanley. The Australians failed to play the one trump card which they held, namely the concessions which they had already promised the United Kingdom in order to facilitate UK-US trade negotiations, and as a result they were forced back on British benevolence.[69] This was not forthcoming, nor could it have been expected.

R.G. Menzies had conceded that the Australian Tariff Board had 'misinterpreted Article X of the Ottawa Agreement in Australia's favour; he was in effect now asking the British to do the same by deleting the obligation on the Australian Parliament to give effect to all Tariff Board Reports.[70] The British refused even to entertain that possibility and suggested a compromise which would have substituted a list of specific preferences on special items for Tariff Board proposals, but this came to nothing when the Australians discovered that they would be much worse off. The Australians then pressed for an expanding share of the British market on the grounds that it had been agreed at Ottawa. It had not. Except in the case of meat, where the concession made was for the expanding share of imports and not of the British market, the Dominions were expected to compete for their share of the British market with British producers and also with those foreign countries which were prepared to absorb the preferential duties. 'The logical outcome of the Australian requests', according to the President of the Board of Trade, was 'that the Empire should establish a closed economy in which the Dominions would provide the agriculture and the United Kingdom the industry. He imagined that no one would want that.'[71]

68 Ibid. **69** Banks Amery to Liesching, 4 July 1938, DO 35, 750/01/65, PRO. **70** Notes of meeting between United Kingdom and Australian Ministers, 17 June 1938, DO 35/759/01/64, PRO. Article X stipulated that the Australian Tariff Board should give the United Kingdom 'full opportunity of reasonable competition on the basis of the relative costs of economical and efficient production'. **71** Meeting between Australian and United Kingdom Ministers and officials, 14 June, 1938,

By 30 June 1938 the negotiations had become deadlocked and had it not been for another timely intervention by Bruce, the discussions could have broken down irretrievably. The result was the drafting of the 'Memorandum of Conclusions' which were little more than polite exchanges of goodwill between the two parties and of laudable but innocuous aspirations which no one could deny, because of the generalities in which they were couched.[72]

Yet the Australian public accepted this outcome. The *Sydney Morning Herald* informed its readers that 'the special value of the talks lies not in any concrete result but in a wider mutual understanding', while the Melbourne *Argus* refused to be dismayed at the failure to revise the Ottawa Agreement because the latter 'had been most valuable to Australia'.[73] However, in London, the *Daily Express* was at its caustic best in exposing the inanities of the final communiqué. It accused the Cabinet of having allowed the negotiations to break down 'rather than nullify pacts with foreign countries'.

The Australians had been allowed to hang about London for three months while the British were too preoccupied with foreign affairs to take enough interest in the British Empire – a prominent Australian in London [unnamed] had said to the *Daily Express* correspondent that 'The British Ministers went into the talks in the spirit of sheer hard bargaining' – with no 'all-one-Empire-family' spirit at all.[74] The British had been doing that since 1932, but the Australians failed to recognise it, or, if they did, tried to convince themselves otherwise. The Australian public had been led up a blind alley so that it was not prepared for failure in London. As a result, platitudes were accepted as substitutes for real progress in commercial negotiations. However, Ministers were becoming sceptical. In a conversation with the United Kingdom acting High Commissioner on 15 July 1938, Lyons had spoken pessimistically of the difficulties he foresaw when the delegates returned. Page, at last, came to realise that their perceptions of Empire trade were ill-founded when in an introspective moment, he wrote in July 1938:

> I set out my view in this way because I cannot persuade myself that the differences now existing between the British Ministers and ourselves are mere differences of draftsmanship. I regard them as reflecting utterly opposed views upon the commercial and industrial development of Australia as a British country.[75]

1667/430/B/67, AA. 72 Cmd 5805. 73 Quoted in DO 35, 750/01/9, PRO. 74 *Daily Express*, 25 July 1938. 75 Memo, 7 July 1938, Page papers, NLA.

He was right. But what was indeed surprising was that it took him and his Cabinet colleagues so long to realise that. The memory of the Ottawa success was slow to fade so that even the rebuffs of 1935 and 1936 did not deflect the Australian delegation from its disastrous course at the 1938 renegotiation of the Ottawa Agreement. The 1938 debacle exposed the fragility of the Empire link. Tangible concessions involving an infringement of national interests were neither entertained nor conceded. Only the sentiment survived, and that had never been in dispute. Throughout the 1930s, Australia believed that imperial sentiment leading to a Commonwealth economic policy guaranteed economic gains, while Britain considered that imperial sentiment was a substitute for economic concessions. In both cases, however, protestations of Empire loyalty served the same purpose of deflecting attention from their own sectional interests.

9

The Australian Department of Trade and the EEC, 1956–1961

The lines of Australia's response to post-1956 trade developments had been set as far back as 1932, following the success of the Australian negotiators at the Ottawa Conference. The Department of Trade, the successor to these negotiators, wholly endorsed the approach taken at Ottawa and were convinced that such an approach would continue to pay dividends for years to come, thereby placing Australian trade policy within an Ottawa time warp that was ultimately to prove quite sterile. John McEwen, the Minister for Trade, believed that the tried technique of bartering trade preferences was still the answer in 1956 to all Australia's trading problems.

The success of the 1956 renegotiation of the Ottawa agreement, which confirmed Australia's traditional access to the British market without having to concede as many preferences as hitherto in its own market to British exporters, opened new fields for McEwen and his staff. Now the Ottawa system could be extended to non-Commonwealth countries, to the mutual benefit of Australia and what 'fortunate' country it chose to solicit. However, for that design to work, it was vital that an international free trade system be promoted. There was no country more dedicated to the concept of free trade than Australia, as long as it did not apply to itself. Australia would only benefit from preferential trade if its customers in its preferential markets were forced to operate on free trade terms, preferences being only effective when selective. McEwen readily endorsed the 1952 Commonwealth collective approach which sought to broaden Commonwealth trade to include dollar area countries, and which thereby implied liberalizing world trade. Nevertheless, when an independent British Commonwealth Committee examined the progress of the scheme in 1958 it found that 'so far as the reduction of discrimination against dollar imports is concerned, Australia has tended to lag behind other Commonwealth countries' because the 'Australian licensing system remains sharply discriminatory against dollar area imports'.[1] The formation of GATT in 1947

1 A4926/XMI, vol. 47, National Archives of Australia, Canberra (AA).

was a windfall for Australia. Recalcitrant countries could now be hauled before that body and forced to purge their anti-liberal misdemeanours.[2] But not Australia. From the outset McEwen made it quite clear that Australia's existing discriminatory preferences were exempt from GATT.[3] Then, in 1958, when about to court non-Commonwealth countries with preferential baits, he was emphatic that 'negotiations with European countries and with the countries of South-East Asia would be broadly outside GATT'.[4] Thus, with the rest of the world moving towards freer trading and with Australia commanding an arsenal of preferences that could now be spread more widely, McEwen confided to his Cabinet colleagues in 1957 that the time was ripe for a major breakthrough in Australia's external trade.[5] He did not foresee or anticipate the impact which the creation of the EEC in 1957 would have on world trade or the way in which existing trade patterns would be transformed.

So accustomed had McEwen and his government colleagues become to the existence of the Commonwealth trading bloc that they were totally blind to the possibility of a rival bloc or blocs appearing. They were convinced that the Commonwealth bloc would remain the sole trading entity in the world, with Britain at its centre and Australia basking in the security which it provided. Those outside that privileged sphere were relegated to mere shadow boxers waiting for a partner of substance to emerge from the Commonwealth to take issue with them – Australia itself being among the more eligible. Thus, when confronted first by the six EEC countries, then by a possible seventeen-member Free Trade Area, next by the seven EFTA countries, then by a possible Nordic Common Market, and finally by the possibility of a Common Market for Latin America, McEwen and his Department were, to say the least, confused if not totally disorientated. R.W.B. Clarke of the British Treasury wrote to Sir Henry Lintott of the Commonwealth Relations Office in November 1957 that he had got the impression from Sir Edwin McCarthy, the Australian High Commissioner in London, that in Canberra there existed 'quite considerable confusion and indeed chaos in the Australian administration on this series of questions'. He went so far as to suggest either that the British Trade Commissioner in Canberra be recalled and trained to instruct the Australians on the intricacies of the EEC, or that Australian civil servants be sent to London 'for two or three weeks to receive indoctrination first hand and then to return and for this process to be repeated every few months'.[6] This did not

2 McEwen's Cabinet Submission, 12 September 1957, A4926/XMI, vol. 34, AA. 3 Minutes of Interdepartmental Meeting on the European Common Market and Free Trade Area, held in Department of Trade, 20 June 1957, A1838/2 791/4/11, Pt. 3, AA. 4 10 July 1958, A4926/XM, vol. 23, AA. 5 21 February 1957, A571 56/1237, Pt. 3, AA. 6 28 November 1957, DO 35/8383,

eventuate. When questioned in the Senate nearly two years later about the implications for Australia of the Common Market, Senator Spooner, Leader of the Government in the Senate, confessed that he 'experienced difficulty in answering questions relating to the European Common Market because of its complexities'. He then referred to eight countries being involved, although he could only recollect the names of six.[7]

It was galling for McEwen and his colleagues that just when the pattern of international trade with all its inherent contradictions seemed to favour Australia, the terms changed. However, because of tradition and also because of an inability to understand or cope with the altered environment, the Department of Trade did not change, preferring instead to follow proven paths, despite the altered international trading topography. For that reason all Australia's efforts to cope with such a novel situation were doomed to failure, and indeed could not have been expected to succeed. Exchanges of preferences on a bilateral basis found scant support in the trading environment of the mid-1950s.

McEwen's first response to the establishment of the EEC was to have it dismantled. He dispatched a note to Brussels in the Australian government's name, condemning the creation of an exclusive trading bloc in Europe sharing preferences among themselves to the exclusion of outside suppliers,[8] failing to acknowledge that 'the Six' were in many ways merely refining the Ottawa system itself. In that note, he deplored 'the level of the common external tariff and the administration of quantitative restrictions and other non-tariff controls on trade'.[9] The EEC ignored McEwen. He next resorted to GATT, and again, on his own initiative, sought to haul the Six before a 'special session of that body'. This was also unsuccessful, mainly because GATT was not prepared to oppose the EEC and took refuge behind procedural and technical barriers. This was despite the fact, that according to the Sub-Committee of the Commonwealth Liaison Committee on European Trade Relations, there was 'no doubt of the incompatibility of a great deal of what the EEC had in mind with Article XI of GATT' (or for that matter with Article XXIV 5a, which 'required that the duties of the common tariff proposed by countries forming a Customs Union shall not on the whole be higher than the general incidence of duties applicable in the constituent territories prior to its formation').[10]

In fact, most of the EEC countries had already managed to opt out of their obligations under GATT. Germany, for example, was 'unwilling to promise

Public Record Office, Kew, London (PRO). 7 Australian Senate, 30 April 1959. 8 A1838/2 791/4/11, Pt. 2, AA. 9 A1209/23 57/5119, Pt. 1, AA. 10 Report of the Sub-Committee on European Trade Relations, August 1959, A1838/2 724/1/9/2, Pt. 2, AA.

any date for the removal of the restrictions in respect of basic agricultural products, a range of manufactured foodstuffs made from these and a range of fruit and vegetables'. Instead it merely pledged at the fourteenth session of GATT in May 1959 'to use her best endeavours to remove such restrictions at the earliest possible date and meanwhile endeavour to improve conditions of access to the German market for all contracting parties'.[11] Luxembourg was recognized to have special problems because of its very small area and 'was accorded a waiver of indefinite duration'. France and Italy had been granted 'waivers' from GATT obligations because of balance of payments difficulties at the ninth session in March 1955.[12] Belgium and the Netherlands, 'while ceasing to claim balance of payments justification for restrictions', nevertheless blatantly persisted with their restrictive practices. The fact that in March 1955, at the time the so-called 'hard core waiver decisions' were being negotiated, the US was granted a waiver of indefinite duration and with no effective limitations in respect of the restrictions which it operated as part of its system of agricultural support, obviously weakened the hand of GATT in its dealings with other and smaller countries. It is therefore understandable that the Sub-Committee of the Commonwealth Liaison Committee on European Trade Relations should have concluded in 1959 that 'the progress made in the GATT in dealing individually with the problem of quantitative restrictions on imports of agricultural products into certain individual countries of the EEC has been disappointing and raises doubts about the results which might be expected when other members of the EEC emerge from balance of payments difficulties'. McEwen therefore had to be content with the innocuous outcome of the autumn 1958 thirteenth session of GATT, which merely appointed three committees to investigate the problem – an illuminating case study in the operation of Parkinson's Law, if nothing more. Committee 1 was established to make recommendations for the holding of further GATT conferences or tariff negotiations on a multilateral basis; Committee 2 was charged with examining the problem of agricultural protectionism as it affected international trade in agricultural products; and Committee 3 was concerned 'with other measures for the expansion of trade'.[13]

Having failed to prevent the formation of the EEC, the Australian government reverted to its proven policy of exchanging preferences, using Britain first of all as an agent in negotiations with EFTA, then inviting the Commonwealth to enter into dialogue with the EEC, and finally initiating direct negotiations on its own with individual EEC countries. It was ironic that just after

11 Ibid. 12 Ibid. 13 Ibid.

Australia had cut some of its strings with Britain following the 1956 renegotiation of the Ottawa Agreement, it should find itself once more on its old mentor's lap. However, McEwen believed that the EEC could only be contained and Australian markets in Europe protected if Britain could entice the six into a wider European arrangement from which agriculture was excluded. In a speech to the Liberal Party Council in October 1957, Menzies highlighted the advantages of a seventeen-member Free Trade Area, indicating that 'if the scope of the EFTA is confined to industrial goods, almost all the Commonwealth preferences can be maintained and at the same time the essentials of association with the European Economic Community can be achieved'.[14] So enamoured were the Australians with the possibility of the 17–member Free Trade Area that McEwen himself was prepared to make agricultural concessions, albeit minor ones, to ensure its success.[15]

This initiative also came to nought. Foreshadowing de Gaulle's dramatic intervention in January 1963, the French soon pulled the carpet from under the British. In a broadcast of November 1958, the French Minister for Information, Monsieur Soustelle, announced that 'France was not prepared to consider the formation of a Free Trade area on the basis of the British proposals'.[16] This the Australian Department of External Affairs interpreted as a clear indication of the divergence between those inside and outside the EEC on the political as distinct from the economic targets of the Common Market. McEwen was palpably disappointed, leading to a temporary cooling in British-Australian relations. When the United Kingdom raised the matter of a separate EFTA of seven countries, Australia's initial response was to distance itself from any new negotiations. At a meeting of Commonwealth officials in London in May 1959, the Australian representative informed the British 'that the position now so far as we are concerned is one of a "clean slate"'.[17] The fact that the EEC would not be party to these new negotiations was a further reason to engage another body such as the seven in pursuing that objective. Instead McEwen proposed that the Commonwealth itself be invited to assist the British in its dealings with the EEC.

Again, McEwen was to be frustrated – not because of EEC opposition, but rather because of Britain's and certain other Commonwealth countries' objections. The initiative had come from the New Zealanders and in welcoming

14 R.G. Menzies, Address to the Liberal Party Council, 21 October 1957, DO 35/8382, PRO. **15** Cabinet Meeting, 17 September 1957, A4926/XM1, vol. 34, AA. **16** Department of External Affairs to Australian High Commissioner, London, January 1960, A1838/2 81/3/2, Pt. 5, AA. **17** McEwen's submission to Cabinet, 8 June 1959, A1838/2 724/1, Pt. 14, AA.

their move McEwen had informed the cabinet in June 1959 that he was attracted by 'some form of Commonwealth association with the European Community which might involve some modification in Commonwealth preferences in return for better access to European markets'.[18] He next cabled Menzies, then in London, 'to put to the U.K. the idea that there should be a thorough examination of the possibility of negotiations between the Commonwealth and European countries'.[19] He could well have anticipated a frosty response from the British to that proposal. During the seventeen-member Free Trade Area negotiations in 1957, the British refused Australia 'a voice in the negotiating arena' because, according to Sir Edwin McCarthy, 'they, the British, fear that to allow Commonwealth countries to get too close to the EFTA negotiating body might embarrass the U.K. in their negotiations'.[20] McEwen was to experience a similar rejection in 1959. He reported to his cabinet that outside of New Zealand 'other Commonwealth countries have not given it wholehearted support'.[21] In fact the United Kingdom and Canada were positively hostile to the idea, with the United Kingdom advising that the 'outer Commonwealth should look after their own interests vis-à-vis the six through the GATT and direct negotiations with the six'.[22] So much for Commonwealth cohesion or British sympathy or support for Australia's trading dilemma.

There can be no doubting McEwen's resentment or even pique at that rebuff. His cherished preferences were no longer being appreciated, and McEwen himself was left in the role of the unrequited suitor. His attitude towards EFTA hardened and he informed cabinet that 'at least at this stage he was not prepared to give it any general blessing'. More surprisingly, he was now opposed to 'a wider free-trade area if it eventuated'.[23] He even questioned the legality of the EFTA in GATT since some features of the EFTA draft plan appeared to be just as much in conflict with GATT as 'those features of the Rome Treaty which we have been attacking'.[24] Thus with his 'preferences' rejected by Britain, rejected by EFTA and also rejected by the Commonwealth, McEwen had no option but to solicit individual EEC countries directly. They also rejected him. The only country even to acknowledge his gesture was Germany, but it only offered to listen further to Australian objections in the event of German discrimination against Australian goods.[25]

Thus, by the time of Britain's momentous decision in July 1961 to join the Common Market itself, Australia found itself stuck in a series of blind alleys

18 Ibid. **19** McEwen to Menzies, 4 June 1959, A1838/2 724/1, Pt. 14, AA. **20** Sir Edwin McCarthy to Canberra, 16 July 1957, A1838/2 791/4/11, Pt. 3, AA. **21** McEwen's submission to Cabinet, 16 September 1959, A5818/2, vol. 8, AA. **22** Ibid. **23** Ibid. **24** Ibid. **25** A1838/2

where it was being marginalized internationally. Assessed in terms of the personnel involved, in distances travelled, in the number of reports produced, in the hours spent at conferences and especially in the frustration of all concerned, not to mention the monetary cost, the price was indeed high. However, what was worse was that Australia's traditional bargaining tool, the exchange of preferences, was being exposed as a paper tiger, and the Department of Trade could not countenance any other approach.

All this begs the basic question: was Australian trade really threatened by these European developments? It must be made clear that Australian preferences in the British market were not at stake during this period, even if Australian suspicions on that score were never fully allayed by British assurances. In a series of public statements, British ministers confirmed the Ottawa preferential system. As early as September 1956 the British Chancellor of the Exchequer advised the Australians that 'UK interests outside Europe, particularly with the Commonwealth, meant that the UK could not in any circumstances join the European Customs Union'.[26] At the Commonwealth Prime Ministers' Meeting in June 1957, Thorneycroft stated that it was the 'firm intention of the United Kingdom government not to agree to include agriculture' in the proposed Free Trade Area, and that that 'had always been made plain to the six countries'.[27] In summing up at that conference, Macmillan was even more emphatic when he stated that 'if the essential safeguards [for the Commonwealth] could not be obtained from the [seventeen-member] EFTA, the United Kingdom would be compelled to stand aside from the European arrangement'.[28] Finally, on a visit to Canberra in February 1958, Macmillan re-emphasized that 'it was not the intention of the United Kingdom to make agricultural concessions' to the EEC.[29] Accordingly, Australian concerns throughout this period were with continental Europe, with the six EEC countries in particular, and not with the United Kingdom. Australian trade policy must therefore be assessed on those terms.

The value of Australia's exports to the EEC countries in 1957–58 was £146 million: just short of Canada's total of £150 million and well below the United Kingdom's £500 million. However, of the three countries, Australia sold a higher proportion of its exports to the EEC: 22.3%, as against 15% for the United Kingdom and 9% for Canada. Further, of these exports, Australia obtained free entry for a much larger proportion of its products. 88% of its

724/1/9/2, Pt. 2, AA. **26** A1209/22 57/5119, Pt. 1, AA. **27** Australian High Commissioner in London to Canberra, 4 July 1957, CRSA 1310/1 56/3/1, AA. **28** Ibid. **29** Meeting between Mr Macmillan and Australian Cabinet in Canberra, 11 February 1958, DO 35/8382, PRO.

exports were admitted free of tariffs to the EEC, as against 22% for Canada, the main reason being that wool and sheepskins, which accounted for the bulk of Australian exports, were not subject to tariffs in the EEC. Thus, at most, only 12% of Australia's exports to the EEC were affected by possible tariff restrictions. Even then, the Sub-Committee of the Commonwealth Liaison Committee on European Trade Relations discounted a portion of the 12%, arguing that 'in 1957–58 there were grounds for anxiety for Australian exports totalling only £8.3 million, representing approximately 5% of her total exports to the EEC', whereas in previous years there would have been grounds for anxiety for approximately '9.1% of Australian total exports to the EEC'. By far the largest share of these problematic exports to the EEC was accounted for by barley and wheat. Australian exports of barley to the EEC in 1957–58 amounted to £3.1 million, or 41% of Australian barley exports to the world. Greater concern was expressed about the future of wheat exports, even though in 1957–58 Australia exported no wheat to the EEC countries. The average of the three previous years was approximately £4 million, about 10% of total Australian world exports of wheat. This anxiety about wheat appears to have sprung from the German 29% *ad valorum* duty on Australian wheat, contrary to the GATT binding rate of 20%. Thus it should be apparent that only a small minority of Australian exports were threatened by EEC developments. In fact the bulk of them could possibly benefit.

McEwen himself was forced to admit in a Cabinet submission of 13 May 1960 that only £15 million of Australia's 1958–59 exports to the EEC were affected by EEC tariffs: wool, sheepskins, lead, zinc and metals were not subject to any duty under EEC proposals. McEwen accordingly conceded that 'our trade is unlikely to be greatly affected'.[31] On the contrary, the Commonwealth Liaison Committee on European Trade Relations concluded that 'exports of wool and sheepskins to the EEC countries can be expected to increase if the creation of the EEC leads to higher living standards and hence to a growing demand for the raw materials of the textile industries'.[32] Even in 1948–49 EEC countries were buying 37% of Australian wool as against 34% by Britain, with Japan taking 29%. The value of Australian greasy wool exports to the United Kingdom in 1956–7 was £106 million; to the EEC countries it was £170 million. In 1948–9 wool exports accounted for 42% of all exports. In 1951 they were 64%, and in 1963 they were 34%.[33] Thus any

30 These and the following statistics are to be found in A1838/2 724/1/9/2, Pt. 2, AA. 31 McEwen's Cabinet submission, 13 May 1960, A5818/2, vol. 16, AA. 32 A1838/2 724/1/9/2, Pt. 2, AA. 33 Quoted in J.G. Crawford, *Australian trade policy, 1942–1966* (1968) pp. 574–5. Also, Aus-

improvement in the sales of wool and sheepskins would have had a major impact on the Australian balance of trade.

These possibilities were not lost on the Prime Minister's Department, the only Australian government department to take issue with the Department of Trade. As early as February 1957, even before the signing of the Treaty of Rome, the Prime Minister's Department had raised strong objections to the Department of Trade's line of action. In a letter to the Secretary of the Department of Trade, A.S. Brown, Secretary of the Prime Minister's Department, upbraided him for his department's unilateral response to the Common Market proposals of the Messina power countries. 'We consider', he wrote, 'that a government to government message was of such significance that it would have been preferable for it to have been discussed in cabinet'. The message itself, he suggested, 'conveyed the impression that we were inclined to take a selfish viewpoint wherever our interests were concerned', which in his view was misguided because 'we cannot exclude the possibility that at some later date in these developments we might be prepared to overlook some possible short-term losses in markets in the interests of contributing to the development of a strong and stable European Community'. He was also critical of the Department of Trade's recourse to GATT, which he considered 'overemphasised'. Inevitably, in his view, 'GATT will be called on to pass judgement on the plan but it would be unfortunate if before we had resolved our overall attitude there should be any possibility of the plan bogging down in a special session of the contracting parties where there could be some danger of losing sight of the fundamental purpose of the plan'.[34] In his subsequent submission to the Prime Minister, Brown was even more emphatic. He stressed that 'the political strategic aspect and the wider trade aspect should not be neglected. Even on the narrower aspect of trade in agricultural commodities, the risks do not seem to be very substantial'. In respect of GATT he advised that Australia 'should encourage effective liaison with the community but not endeavour to put them through the hoops'.[35]

The Prime Minister's Department followed up this attack in March 1957 with a trenchant memorandum written by Peter Lawler, which accused the Department of Trade of being fixed myopically on the agricultural aspects of the EEC, and of ignoring the welcome which the United States and Canada had given it on political grounds and also the other trade advantages which in the Prime Minister's Department's view did exist in the new arrangements. The Department of Trade, it alleged, was

tralian Bureau of Statistics, *Overseas trade, 1956–7*, Bulletin No.54, p. 539. 34 A.S. Brown to J.G. Crawford, 5 Feb 1957, AA, A1838/2 719/4/11, Pt. 2. 35 A4926/XM, vol. 23, AA.

'moping with imagined fears about wilting trade opportunities'. While Lawler acknowledged that the EEC was largely self-sufficient in certain agricultural products – for example supplying 84% of its own bread grain needs, 75% of its beef and veal and 90% of its butter – it was not self-sufficient in certain agricultural products – it was not self-sufficient in the commodities that most affected Australia namely wool and sheepskins. The Prime Minister's Department calculated that 'a 2% increase in wool sales' would be the 'equivalent of a 10% increase in Australian sales of other items to the six'. If the European Community and the Free Trade Area lead to economic expansion in Europe, that should enhance Australia's overall export opportunities even if 'a few marginal items might get hit'. Anyway, it argued, 'the changes involved in the Common Market will be staggered over a number of years'. Accordingly, the Prime Minister's Department cautioned against confrontation with the EEC; it recommended a 'nod and a wink' approach to GATT surveillance on the grounds that 'if we faced similar pressures, for example, the sale of New Zealand butter in Australia, would we be as enthusiastic about GATT investigations?' Finally it argued that Australia should offer 'a public and Free Trade Area', as both the US and Canada had already done.[36]

In the opinion of the Prime Minister's Department, the future lay with the regional economic blocs then appearing all over the world. Lawler later argued that 'there was no mistaking that the regional approach to a solution of trade payments problems was in the ascendancy. The European Economic Community was established. The Free Trade Area was being devised; the Nordic Common Market stood ready to be put into operation and serious work was proceeding on a Common Market for Latin America'.[37] Accordingly, the Prime Minister's Department strongly recommended that Australia follow New Zealand's example and associate itself with a widely expanded Free Trade Area, or if that failed with the EEC itself.[38] The Department also recommended that Australia should accredit an official to the EEC Commission in Brussels.[39] While the Prime Minister's Department agreed that its approach was somewhat unorthodox, it maintained that 'as our present approach is certain to be unfruitful and even damaging there is therefore merit in seeking an alternative' – with 'closer economic co-operation with Europe as the best means of promoting our trade and other interests'.[40]

36 Ibid. **37** Ibid., 11 July 1958. **38** 10 July 1958, A4926/XM, vol. 23, AA. **39** N.L. Hibbs (British Trade Commissioner, Canberra) to Miss D.M.Wilde (Board of Trade), 20 August 1959, DO35/8383, PRO. **40** 10 July 1958, A4926/XM, vol. 23, AA.

Emanating from such an important source as the Prime Minister's Department, it might have been expected that these ideas would have carried some weight. The opposite, however, was the case, for the very simple reason that the Prime Minister does not appear to have had much influence himself. On trade matters, Menzies was no more than McEwen's spokesman, and that was accordingly reflected in the lowly ranking of this department in that sphere. As has been noted, McEwen acted as if he alone was the Australian government – a sort of political organ grinder. He composed and sent aide-memoires in the government's name without consulting anybody, and he even instructed Menzies on the appropriate responses when the latter was in London. He was to continue to do so with even greater frequency in the early 1960s.

Equally influential was McEwen's departmental head, John G. Crawford. Writing to Clarke of the Treasury in December 1957, Sir Edgar Coagan of the Board of Trade noted that 'the key to the problem at the Australian end is to carry Jack Crawford with us'. He advised that the British civil service should take the unprecedented step of 'sending personal messages to Jack Crawford, in addition to any message which is sent to the Government', because of his belief that Crawford 'reacts quite especially to direct personal messages'.[41] This view was endorsed by Sir Henry Lintott of the Commonwealth Relations Office, who in a letter, also to Clarke, confirmed that he agreed 'that Crawford is the key to our problem at the Australian end'.[42] Harry Gray, the British Trade Commissioner in Canberra, also maintained that Crawford had been upset by other government departments being involved in trade matters, especially by the 'recent decision to hold regular meetings with Commonwealth High Commissioners in London'.[43] The outcome was that R.W.B. Clarke wrote to Lintott at the end of December 1957 recommending that Sir Frank Lee and Sir Rasley Rowan be appointed letter writers to Crawford, because of their personal relations with him.[44] However, Lintott now demurred. 'Such a course', he said, 'was likely to make our relations with other governments unnecessarily complicated.' In addition, 'it could easily create jealousies amongst those to whom messages were not sent'.[45] McEwen and Crawford did not need these assurances; their dominance in the Australian public service was unassailable. At an interdepartmental meeting in June 1957 all departments, including External Affairs and Primary Industry, endorsed the Depart-

41 Sir Edgar Coagan to R.W.B. Clarke, 2 December 1957, DO35/8383, PRO. 42 Sir Henry Lintott to R.W.B. Clarke, 10 December 1957, DO35/8383, PRO. 43 Sir Edgar Coagan to R.W.B. Clarke, 2 December 1957 in which he refers to Gray's information, DO35/8383, PRO. 44 R.W.B. Clarke to Sir Henry Lintott, 19 December 1957, DO35/8383, PRO. 45 Sir Henry Lintott to R.W.B. Clarke, 30 December 1957, DO35/8383, PRO.

ment of Trade's position, although the Treasury was ambivalent, recommending that Australia should take a passive role in respect of the proposed Treaty of Rome, 'listening' rather than intervening.[46]

Accordingly there was no effective check on the direction of Australian trade policy between 1956 and 1961. The Prime Minister's Department did not matter. Years later, in his documentary history of *Australian Trade Policy*, Crawford was to question the 'competency' of these observers, who in his view were 'ignorant of further technological developments in European agriculture so that in cereals, sugar and dairy products, imports could be expected to diminish greatly and even disappear'.[47] Again he missed the point made by his critics, who had never denied that fact, but who had placed these products within the context of total EEC imports, where the losses would be compensated for by the gains. More convincing, however, was the political argument, not alluded to by Crawford: namely that these minority crops were located in politically sensitive regions in Australia. This was the perceptive conclusion of J.D.B. Miller in 1976, who wrote that 'Rural electorates all over Australia but especially in sugar, fruit and dairying areas had an overwhelming interest in preserving special access'. For the Country Party these special interests 'could be represented as a matter of life and death since if that Party were unable to ensure them the special protection they had been accustomed to, there would be little reason for the separate existence of a rural non-Labour Party and the Liberal Party might overrun what had formally been Country Party strongholds'.[48]

Thus the pattern of Australian trade responses was set by a combination of tradition, the blinkered vision of McEwen, Crawford and their departmental officials, and sectional political interests. It was accordingly a partial response that tended to ignore the wider implications, and so, as has been seen, was doomed to failure. But because it had been hyped up as Australia's response to a greater challenge than in fact existed, the disillusion was even more pronounced. This also provides some explanation for the near panic in government circles in Australia in July 1961 when Britain itself decided to join the Common Market, thereby posing a genuine threat to Australian export trade. Menzies was to refer to that as the greatest challenge of his political career, even dwarfing the Second World War. Government departments were left floundering. The legacy of the shadow boxing of the previous six years that had been mis-

46 Interdepartmental Meeting on the European Common Market and Free Trade Area, held in Department of Trade, 20 June 1957, A1838/2 791/4/11, Pt. 3, AA. 47 Crawford, *Australian trade policy*, pp. 272–3. 48 J.D.B. Miller, *The EEC and Australia* (1976) p. 78.

taken for the real thing now came to haunt the Department of Trade, initially nearly paralysing the government response to these new and more serious developments. This panic is neatly captured in a memorandum of July 1961 which recommended that Australia's response to Britain's intention to seek membership of the EEC should be 'to avoid either saying or giving the impression that we can be counted on ultimately for support as long as a few recognisable concessions are made in our direction and on the other to avoid saying or giving the impression that we are opposed almost immovably to the initiative by Great Britain – for the present we reserve our position. We are not supporting. We are not opposing. And we are not neutral or indifferent. We will have views, but not yet'.[49] A species of levitating diplomacy that was entirely original.

49 Memorandum, 6 July 1961, A571/95 1961/791, Pt. 9, AA.

10

The British Commonwealth and the EEC, 1960–1963

In a letter to Robert Menzies in February 1962, Harold Macmillan reflected nostalgically on what he termed the old Commonwealth where, 'they all felt they belonged to the same intimate family. They had the king or queen as the object of their personal loyalty and the conferences were agreeable as well as valuable. There was no dispute – there was interesting discussion, an opportunity of meeting old friends, the charm of the royal presence and all on a scale that was like a small and pleasant house party,'[1] a view endorsed even more fulsomely by Menzies in his address to the Australian Club dinner in June of that year when he referred to his friend Harold Macmillan and himself being members of a Commonwealth 'where roots have been nurtured in the soil of cooperation and affection and loyalty'.[2] In fact, Mr Diefenbaker when elaborating in the Canadian House of Commons on 'how much the Commonwealth meant to them' attributed the concept to John A. MacDonald, the founder of his own conservative party.

Such observations border on the musings normally reserved for the slumbering brigade in city clubs and totally ignore the semi-paralysis of the final days of the Ottawa Conference when insults were freely exchanged 'which' Neville Chamberlain, 'would never had imagined it possible he should have borne'.[3] These were recalled by Edward Heath in August 1962 when he described a particularly fractious meeting with the Australians on temperate foodstuffs as being 'less contentious than that which had led to the conclusion of the Ottawa agreements'.[4] But that was 30 years ago; what of the disharmony caused by Curtin's unilateral actions during World War I and the split in Commonwealth ranks during the Suez crisis, or even more recently the preferential treatment to Common Market countries holding sterling balances to the detriment of the old Commonwealth that Australia only discovered by

1 Harold Macmillan to R.G. Menzies, 8 February 1962, Prem 11/3644, Public Record Office, London (PRO). 2 R.G. Menzies at Australia Club Dinner, Savoy, London, 12 June 1964, A 1838/2. 727/4, p 30, Australian Archives, Canberra, AA. 3 G. Whiskard to E.J. Harding, 19 August 1932, DO35, 121/6, PRO. 4 British Cabinet Meeting, 22 August 1962, CAB 1287, PRO.

chance when investigating the currency implications of Britain's membership of the EEC: it was quite a jolt for Harold Holt, the Australian Treasurer, to learn that while Australian holdings of sterling were subject to all the risks of devaluation, Common Market countries dealings in sterling were not.[5]

It is apparent therefore that Macmillan, Menzies and Diefenbaker exaggerated the cohesion of the Commonwealth and understated the strains which these various developments had placed on Commonwealth relationships – no doubt influenced by the solidarity still evident as late as 1961 and aware that until then, differences arose only respecting the appropriate responses external challenges such as the Depression or German or Japanese aggression. The currency anomaly should have been an augury of things to come but it was lost on the rest of the Commonwealth either through lack of vigilance or gullibility. Britain's decision in July 1961 to commence proceedings with a view to joining the EEC was another matter; now not only was there an alternate grouping on the horizon that posed a threat to the Commonwealth's own neat trading arrangements, but on this occasion one of its own members, in fact its founder and gravitational epicentre, was apparently contemplating joining. The enemy was no longer outside the walls but was firmly entrenched within; and neither Australia nor Canada had anticipated that Britain would default on its own organization, to the benefit of a potential competitor.

This was difficult to comprehend; Australia and Canada had witnessed Britain's attempt to circumnavigate the EEC, either by the creation of an enlarged European organization that would dilute the dominance of any one group or later, when unsuccessful, by the establishment of an alternative, if looser, smaller body that would be more accommodating of third parties. Throughout these proceedings, Australia and Canada had been assured that their needs would be secured and now, contrary to these affirmations, Britain herself was opting to join the enemy and place the interests of the Commonwealth at risk. Australia and Canada would not concede that Britain had no alternative, that Britain was as reluctant as themselves to enter into a liaison with the EEC but as the EEC had been established and was going from strength to strength, Britain believed that it would ignore it at its peril. While Macmillan in his August 1961 speech to the House of Commons may have emphasized the political advantage of maintaining unity in Western Europe and thus avoiding another German conflict, and also of using membership 'to induce other countries to adopt liberal policies', the immediate danger and thus the determining factor in the British government's decision to investigate membership of the

5 Position paper by Australian Treasury, 26 June 1961, A 5818/vol. 28, AA.

EEC was the growing economic threat from a powerful competitor on its own doorstep. Macmillan may well have pointed to the positive benefits that would 'rub off' from 'association with a powerful economic entity' but he was much more concerned lest Britain decline, albeit by default, while the EEC prospered. Thus the EEC was as much an embarrassment and an inconvenience for Britain as it was for the Commonwealth; the only difference being that while the rest of the Commonwealth could temporarily ignore it, Britain could not.[6]

While the United Kingdom continued to provide assurances throughout the EEC negotiation that Commonwealth interests would be catered for, it became increasingly obvious, not least to the likes of the Australians, Canadians and New Zealanders that these were shelved once Britain's own interests were threatened. For example, Mr Macmillan told the House of Commons in May 1961 that 'satisfactory arrangements [. . .] in respect of the interests of our fellow members of the Commonwealth [. . .] are prerequisite of any closer association with the European Economic Community'.[7] While Anthony Eden in a speech in June of that year asserted that 'no British government can enter into engagements which do not fully honour its obligations to those who stood by us in good times and bad with a loyalty beyond compare in the history of the world'.[8] In the communiqué issued after Mr Duncan Sandy's visit to Australia in July 1961, it was stated that 'he assured the Australian government that the British government fully shared its concern to maintain the long established flow of trade between their two countries. If negotiations took place, the intention would be to secure special arrangements to protect these important trading interests.'[9] He went even further in his address later that year to the annual conference of the Conservative Party where he reiterated that 'both the Prime Minister and I and other Ministers have given the most solemn undertakings to Parliament that if we cannot secure special arrangements to protect vital Commonwealth interests, then Britain will not join the Common Market'.[10] The British government did not deliver on these guarantees and could not have been expected to do so in view of the intransigence of the six, especially the French.

But these failures do not in any way detract from the genuineness of the British intentions; in cabinet meeting after cabinet meeting, the needs of the

6 H. Macmillan's speech in House of Commons, 2 August 1961 and Selwyn Lloyd's speech to fourth meeting of Commonwealth Economic Consultative Council at Accra, 13 September 1961, CAB/176, PRO. 7 Hansard, 9 May 1961, p. 219. 8 Anthony Eden's speech, 10 June 1961, found in cable 2865, Australian High Commissioner London AA. 9 Communiqué issued in Canberra after Duncan Sandys' visit, 9 July 1961, A 1838/2 727/4, p. 8, AA. 10 Duncan Sandys speaking at the Conservative Party Conference, 10 October 1961.

Commonwealth were highlighted and the commitment of the British government to their achievement, emphasized – Mr Macmillan stated in June 1961 that 'our aim would be to secure for the Commonwealth outlets for their essential products in the community as a whole' and 'we should certainly do our best to maintain as much as we can'.[11] When rebuffed by the six in July 1962, the cabinet concluded that 'we could not accept their present proposals and it would be wrong to try to persuade the other Commonwealth countries to do so',[12] and even when the Commonwealth position appeared hopeless as a result of the persistent rebuffs by the French, Mr Heath informed cabinet that they 'should continue to press for nil tariffs on raw materials and for fair treatment of processed foodstuffs and manufacturers [. . .] for the old Commonwealth'.[13] In fact, in an interview with Mr Whitlam, deputy leader of the Australian Labor Party, in June 1962, Mr Heath indicated that 'if we had not had the Commonwealth but only our own domestic interests to think of, then negotiations would probably have taken little more than a few weeks'.[14] Accordingly, the British failing was not in the sincerity of their promises to the Commonwealth, but in their insistence on their achievement, long after it became obvious that the community would not be moved.

It was unrealistic to expect that Commonwealth countries would accept these assurances while they were witnessing the gradual dismantling of the Ottawa preferential system throughout 1962. In May 1962, the British concurred with the EEC in ending British tariff preferences on manufactured goods from Australia, Canada and New Zealand by 1970, thereby rejecting Australia's proposal for tariff preference quotas.[15] Sandys' much-vaunted promise of 'comparable outlets' for temperate foodstuffs in an enlarged Common Market[16] had been discarded by September 1962 and the problem was transferred to a vaguely defined World Conference on total output and sales of each commodity to be held in 1963, after Britain had been accepted into the EEC. Sandys then had to write to Menzies that 'we are reluctantly forced to the conclusion that this means that there is virtually no prospect of retaining the existing Commonwealth preferences after the transitional period'.[17] The allegedly firm commitment on price policy for temperate products 'that appeared to have been agreed by August 1962' and 'which would offer reasonable opportunities for imports of temperate foodstuffs'[18] and that would also 'be arranged in such a

11 H. Macmillan memo to Cabinet, 21 June 1961, CAB 129, PRO. 12 British cabinet meeting, 31 July 1962, CAB 128, PRO. 13 British cabinet meeting, 27 September 1962, CAB 134/1515, PRO. 14 E. Heath to E.J. Whitlam, 12 June 1962, DO 159/60, PRO. 15 *Australian Financial Times*, 31 May 1962. 16 Duncan Sandys' discussions in Canberra, July 1961, A 1838/2 727/4, p. 8, AA. 17 Duncan Sandys' to R.G. Menzies, 24 July 1962, A 1838/2 727/4, p. 33, AA. 18 British cabinet

way as to avoid a reduction in consumption or the over stimulation of production in the community itself'[19] had also been abandoned by November 1962 in favour of a minimum price. In the case of wheat, the price set was £37 per ton which even Heath said, in his submission to cabinet, was too high because it 'would make it impossible for the community to carry out their assurances and so the provisions and values of July would be shown to be worthless'.[20]

There were a number of conclusions which the Australians and the Canadians could draw from these developments; either the British had misled them with their assurances or the British were incompetent negotiators or the six were totally intransigent – the Australians tended to question British sincerity and also its negotiating abilities while the Canadians suspecting British motives, were still apparently content to rely on the British team in Brussels rather than make direct overtures themselves or seek to participate in these negotiations. Both countries appeared to have underestimated the opposition of the six. Despite their reservations both Australia and Canada still relied on Britain in formulating their responses to Common Market developments so that Britain was invariably blamed when things went wrong. However, by continuing to raise their expectations, Britain itself contributed substantially to their resentments and also ensured that both countries would fail to recognize that Britain naively still hoped to satisfy all interests, its own, the Commonwealth and the six long after these had become more and more incompatible.

Inevitably the first casualty of this perceived subterfuge was trust. Always fragile, especially after the battering at Ottawa, Britain's overtures to Brussels, and especially Edward Heath's opening address, did nothing to allay suspicions. Heath's opening statement in Paris on 10 October 1961 was a straightforward presentation of Britain's and Commonwealth's requirements from membership of the EEC and there was no hidden agenda; however, because of the secrecy surrounding its construction, and the selectivity involved in the fragmented release of excerpts to Commonwealth members, it inevitably aroused totally unwarranted doubts about Britain's motivations. Each party appears to have concluded that there was something sinister in the sections to which it was not privy. The British cabinet had justified this procedure on the spurious grounds that Britain 'should avoid erecting any precedent of having to consult them (Commonwealth and EFTA) before making statements on matters affecting them or of being committed to supply them with copies of any such statements'.[21]

meeting, 22 August 1962, CAB 128, PRO. **19** British cabinet meeting, 31 July 1962, CAB 128, PRO. **20** E. Heath to British cabinet, 26 November 1962, CAB 134/1516, PRO. **21** Meeting of the British Cabinet Common Market Committee, 4 October 1961, CAB 134/1511, PRO.

This was a mistake, especially as the full draft was subsequently leaked by one of the six to the Canadians who duly passed it on to other Commonwealth governments. When the matter was raised in the House of Commons in November, Mr Gaitskell pointed out that it 'is bound to create the impression that you do not trust the Commonwealth governments to keep these things secret. If you hope to carry Commonwealth with you, it is far better to trust them'. 'You may not care about the Commonwealth' he said to Mr Heath 'but we do' and *The Times* considered that 'an error of judgement was committed' though the *Daily Telegraph* considered it 'a leak in a tea cup'.[22] Subsequently the British cabinet had second thoughts about not giving details to all interested parties and decided that thereafter they 'should pay particular attention to keeping up a steady flow of information to them about progress of the negotiations[23] but the damage had been done, with both McEwen and Diefenbaker in particular excessively wary of British pronouncements and actions from there on. For example, while in London in March 1962, Mr McEwen stated that 'he (McEwen) would like to feel that the British trusted them, but that if the British wished to treat the Australian government as opponents, well and good, but he would like to know'.[24] In a report to London in February 1962 Lord Amory, the British High Commissioner in Ottawa said that 'he found Mr Diefenbaker's attitude disturbing' as 'he (Diefenbaker) claims that we are hustling him and showing insufficient regard for Commonwealth interests [. . .] he does not regard any discussions between officials as consultations' – he was also under the impression that 'Mr Macmillan was anxious to avoid a Prime Ministers' Conference presumably because he must have had something to hide.'[25]

Not being sure where they stood in respect to their own future within the British market or within the enlarged Common Market, induced flights of paranoia in both countries that reinforced nationalistic instincts to the detriment of Commonwealth cohesion. As a result, their response to most British overtures was essentially defensive and/or deprecatory while at the same time projecting an image of their own helplessness. Nowhere was that more evident than in their exaggeration of their losses should Britain join the EEC.

Coincidentally, both countries' trade with Britain in 1962 accounted for only approximately 15% to 18% of the value of their total exports though invariably that figure was not alluded to either in their public or private protes-

22 High Commissioner London to Department of External Affairs Canberra, 28 November 1961, A 1209/24 1961/1139, AA. 23 Ibid. 24 Meeting in London between E. Heath and J. McEwen, 21 March 1962, DO 159/57, PRO. 25 British High Commissioner in Canada to Commonwealth Relations Office, undated presumably February or March 1962, DO 159/52, PRO.

tations of strangulation by the British government. Mr McEwen always referred to a much higher amount being in danger; for example in a press interview in March 1962 when his attention was drawn to Lord Chandos's observation that 'only 18% of Australian exports were likely to be concerned' (by the EEC), Mr McEwen curtly retorted that that was 'very dangerous thinking for we have industries here like the canned fruit industry in my own electorate that are 90% dependent upon the UK for their export trade',[26] a theme that was pursued in all Australian submissions. Much was made of the fact that Britain in 1961 purchased over 40% of Tasmanian apple and pear production, took 75% of total wine exports and 57% of total exports of dairy products,[27] but little was made of the dramatic drop in the proportion of Australian exports finding their way to the British market – a drop in ten years of approximately 13% in contrast to the dramatic doubling in exports to Japan during the same period.[28] And if one allows for the fact that wool, hides, skins and metal ores and concentrates which accounted for approximately one-third of Australian trade with the United Kingdom would have had free access to the enlarged Common Market, then only 10–12% of Australian trade was in danger.

And even then, there were potentially compensating factors of enhanced demand especially for the latter commodities from an increasingly prosperous EEC – a prospect that was emphasized by W.E.G. Salter in his September 1961 submission to the Prime Minister[29] and later elaborated on by the Australian Minister of Air, Mr Bury, who, much to his cost, publicly stated in July 1962 that 'the effect of Australia would be limited' from British membership of the EEC, to which Mr McEwen replied that 'he was shocked that a ministerial colleague should publicly undercut the strength of Australia's negotiating position'.[30] Bury lost his job. The 'negotiating position' was more important than the reality. Although Canada only exported 15% of its produce to the UK compared with 60% to the United States in 1959/60 the statistic always cited was the proportion of that 15% which would be affected by United Kingdom entry to the EEC. In a speech in Winnipeg in January 1962, Donald M. Fleming, the Canadian Minister for Finance, stated that 'you will see that of the total Canadian sales of $915m to the United Kingdom in 1960, $691m or 76% could be affected in a greater or lesser degree if the British were to join the Common Market'.[31] This was later translated by Mr Diefen-

26 J. McEwen press interview, 4 March 1962, A 1838/274 727/4, p 25, AA. **27** Departmental paper *Australian exports and the European Economic Community*, 4 April 1962, A 1838/274 727/4, p. 27, AA. **28** Ibid. **29** W.E.G. Salter to R.G. Menzies, 29 August 1961, A 4940/1 C 3368 part 3, AA. **30** J. McEwen, 28 July 1962, A 1838/2 727/4, p 23, p. 33, AA. **31** Speech by Donald M. Fleming at

baker himself in a speech in Montreal on 20 March 1962 to '76% of Canadian exports' that might be affected by 'Britain's entry into the EEC'.[32]

In all these respects, there are similarities in Australian and Canadian perceptions of and responses to Britain's decision to join the EEC – there was the same lack of trust, the same exaggeration of the adverse effects on their trade and the same stridency in their statements. But here the similarities end. From then on Australia was far more aggressive than Canada, insisting on consultation and even involvement at all stages of the negotiations and even demanding that it have independent access to the six. Further it was the Australians and not the Canadians or New Zealanders, that orchestrated opposition to Britain among other Commonwealth countries by means of acerbic notes addressed to them or, more important, by way of personal visits either by Mr Menzies or more usually by Mr McEwen.

Canada, however, demurred to Britain's expertise, preferring to reserve its judgement until the outcome of Britain's negotiations was known. Menzies was, in fact, amazed in June 1962 when it was decided by Britain and the six to phase out preferences on manufacturers to Britain by 1970 that Canada, the most seriously affected, did not protest. In a letter to McEwen he asked, 'how Canada can sit silent under this agreement puzzles me, I have not read that it has yet stirred either Diefenbaker or Pearson to comment'.[33] Further, Canada, as Donald Fleming told the House of Commons in Ottawa in February 1962, did not 'ask for a place at the negotiating table' and the Canadian government did 'not see an occasion for making such a request'.[34] When eventually the British government prevailed on the Canadians to send a token complement of officials to Brussels to monitor progress of the EEC talks, these gentlemen took the task lightly, albeit even flippantly. Mr Latimer, the first such official, began 'by repeating for the record the Canadian line that they regard all their exports to the United Kingdom as being of importance' but then 'made it clear that he was not going to be tiresome about this'.[35] While Jake Warren, another Canadian official at a meeting on agriculture held in London in February 1962, produced 'a cigar and a billy bottle of brandy from his brief case and presented them to the chairman, Mr Bishop, from the Ministry of Agriculture and Fisheries, at a suitable moment'.[36] The prevailing atmosphere and substance of

Winnipeg, 19 January 1962, DO 159/52, PRO. 32 British High Commissioner, Ottawa, to Commonwealth Relations Office, 21 March 1962, DO 159/52, PRO. 33 R.G. Menzies to J. McEwen, 2 June 1962, A 1838/2 274/4, p 30, AA. 34 Extract from House of Commons Debates in Canada, 15 February 1962, DO 159/52, PRO. 35 Note by C.J. Audland, member of the United Kingdom delegation to the Brussels Conference, 14 January 1962, DO 159/52, PRO. 36 J.R.A. Bottomley to K. McGregor, British High Commissioner's Office, 14 February 1962, DO 159/52, PRO.

these British exchanges with the Canadians is, perhaps, best captured by Ms N.K. Fisher of the Board of Trade, following a meeting with Canadian officials: 'in the space of five hours, the Canadian representatives read out the UK tariff. They were ignorant of the facts of their trade, they had no ideas. They preached three sermons, all of them on the same text', and she concluded that 'none who was not actually present could have guessed at the futility of the discussion', and then apologized for 'this failure of imagination'.[37]

The irony, however, was that Britain considered the Canadians far more disruptive, totally unprincipled and, especially in the case of Mr Diefenbaker, totally unpredictable than they did the Australians. Accordingly, throughout the proceedings the United Kingdom tended to fight shy of the Canadians, to view with suspicion their every statement and move and to expect the worst of them especially during the September 1962 Commonwealth Prime Ministers' Conference. With the Australians it was otherwise; Mr Menzies was invariably feted on his many trips to Britain during the negotiations while allowances continued to be made for Mr McEwen's outbursts from which the British invariably exonerated Mr Menzies.

This British antagonism towards Canada owed much to their disgust with the Canadian stance at the Accra Conference of the Commonwealth Economic Consultative Council in September 1961, to their resentment at the reception meted out to Mr Duncan Sandys when he visited Ottawa in July 1961 and finally to their distrust of Mr Diefenbaker. The Canadian delegation at Accra, Mr Fleming, the Canadian Minister for Finance and Mr Hees, the Minister for Trade and Commerce, did not endear themselves to the British representatives, Mr Selwyn Lloyd, Mr Maudling and the Duke of Devonshire, nor did they gain the admiration of the British press, especially Mr Nigel Lawson. The Australian High Commissioner in Accra reported that 'Fleming had made a forceful and uncompromising speech against United Kingdom entry,'[38] while Nigel Lawson accused the Canadians, whom he alleged drafted the Accra communiqué, of a 'deliberate attempt to sabotage Britain's entry altogether', which was consistent, in Lawson's view, with their policy of 'seeing the Commonwealth relationship as a strictly one sided affair'.[39]

Five months after the event Lord Amory, the British High Commissioner in Canada, was still referring to the Canadians' 'violent demarche at Accra'.[40]

37 Report of a meeting with Canadian officials on the future of Common Market negotiations by Ms N.K. Fisher of the Board of Trade, 1 November 1961, DO 164/42, PRO. 38 Australian High Commissioner Accra to Department of Foreign Affairs Canberra, 15 September 1962, A 1838/2 727/4, p 12, AA. 39 *Sunday Telegraph*, 24 September 1961, A 1838/2 727/4, p 13, AA. 40 Lord

However, a reading of the Canadian and Australian speeches at Accra indicate very few differences and, after all, Australia also contributed to and signed the final communiqué. Why then the differences in perception? Obviously if not the content of the speech, it could only have been the mode of delivery coupled with their extra conference activities such as 'handing out their confidential speeches to the press' which, surprisingly, according to the Australians, led to 'genuine irritation with the Canadian approach'[41] especially among the British press corps. Perhaps most important of all was that, unlike the Australians, Mr Fleming at Accra warned that the prevailing method of securing trade was by exchange of trading advantages. Accordingly, if Canada was to lose its trading advantages within the UK it would not be in the spirit of retaliation that it would find it necessary to withdraw reciprocal advantages from the UK in order to use that bargaining power in her search for other markets.[42]

The Australians, at that stage of the negotiations, considered it expedient to keep that option in reserve. The Canadians again incurred Britain's displeasure during Mr Duncan Sandys' well-publicized familiarization trips to Commonwealth capitals in July 1961. In his report on his visits to the British Cabinet, Mr Sandys commented on the 'friendly atmosphere in which the talks were conducted, particularly in New Zealand and Australia'.[43] He made no mention of Canada. This was in spite of the fact that the New Zealanders had made it absolutely 'clear that they would be utterly ruined . . . without making far reaching arrangements' for them and that Australia had steadfastly refused to endorse Britain's entry into the EEC and would go no further than concede that as an independent country, Britain had the right to apply.[44] In a letter to Mr Holyoake, the New Zealand prime minister, following Sandys' visit, Mr Menzies mentioned 'that we had a tussle over the communiqué – Duncan wanted us in the first place not to make any reference to objecting or approving and when we would not settle for that, to say that we neither approved nor disapproved. But we felt that we would not let it go at that. It would represent a state of indifference or neutrality which would not properly represent our position'.[45]

It was therefore the tone of the Canadian response rather than the content that infuriated Britain, as is apparent from Canadian newspaper reports of the

Amory to Joe Garner, 15 February 1962, DO 159/52, PRO. 41 Ibid. 42 Report of Conference proceedings at Accra, 13 September 1961, CAB 133/176, PRO. 43 Duncan Sandys' report to British cabinet, 21 July 1961, CAB 129 – C (61) 111, PRO. 44 Communiqué following Duncan Sandys' visit to Australia, July 1961, A 1838/2 727/4, p. 8, AA. 45 Ibid.

visit; the *Montreal Gazette* stated that the Canadian government's 'reaction to Sandys was frigid', the *Ottawa Citizen* concluded that 'the terse and angry communiqué underlined the deadlock', while the *Globe and Mail* found that 'the tersely worded communiqué was 'the stiffest of the older Commonwealth countries'.[46] Ultimately these criticisms focused on Mr Diefenbaker himself, towards whom, despite his numerous protestations of loyalty to Britain and the Commonwealth, Britain was essentially suspicious or even hostile. In January 1962 he asserted that 'the foundation of the conservative party is close relationship with the British Commonwealth',[47] and again in May of that year when he affirmed that 'I have always been devoted to the Commonwealth',[48] Britain did not believe him. His constant demand for a Commonwealth Conference preferably held in Ottawa,[49] did not find favour, nor was his image enhanced by the barrage of hostile comments, transmitted to Britain by Lord Amory. Sir William Oliver, the corresponding official in Canberra, was much more even-handed.

The *Evening Standard* saw Amory's appointment to Ottawa as 'a ploy to make the Canadians enthusiastic about the market'.[50] And that appeared to be self-fulfilling because in all his reports to the Commonwealth Relations Office or to Mr Macmillan, he invariably spoke of the widespread Canadian support for the EEC, the only exception being the Diefenbaker government. In September 1962 he reported that 'the general attitude towards our Common Market project is understanding and sympathetic [. . .] however criticism of the Canadian government's negative and unconstructive attitude is widespread'.[51] He found Diefenbaker 'irresolute by nature and hyper sensitive to public opinion' who believed that 'Britain was willing to write off the Commonwealth', the prospect of which induced 'an angry and injured tone in him'.[52]

While the *Evening Standard* disputed Amory's claim of universal Canadian support for the EEC, the important point is that he exercised a profound influence on his superiors back in London which undoubtedly reinforced anti-Canadian prejudice already in abundance there. The Commonwealth Relations Office did not trust the Canadian High Commissioner in London, Mr Drew. They alleged that he was having 'a damaging influence on Mr Diefenbaker's thinking' by feeding him information that 'the mass of the peo-

46 Australian High Commissioner Ottawa to Department of External Affairs Canberra, 18 July 1962, A 1838/2 727/4, p. 8, AA. 47 Mr Diefenbaker speaking on 30 January 1962, DO 159/52, PRO. 48 Mr Diefenbaker speaking, 2 May 1962, DO 159/54 PRO. 49 Lord Amory to Commonwealth Relations Office, 26 March 1962, DO 159/53, PRO. 50 *Evening Standard*, 15 June 1962. 51 Lord Amory to Secretary of State for Commonwealth Relations, 6 September 1962, DO 159/54, PRO. 52 Lord Amory to H. Macmillan, 23 March 1962, DO 159/54, PRO.

ple in England and of conservative party supporters in the House and outside disapprove of the government's attempt to negotiate membership of the EEC'.[53] This may well explain why Duncan Sandys should have found Diefenbaker 'uncooperative and obstructive' and intent on making 'things as difficult as possible for us',[54] and far more importantly why Britain should have devoted so much time and energy throughout 1962 cultivating Mr Diefenbaker. Mr Heath, despite his demanding schedule of meetings between London and Brussels, made two visits to Ottawa in January and March, while Prime Minister Macmillan made one in May. With the exception of Duncan Sandys' visit in July 1961, no other British minister visited Australia during the EEC negotiations. They did not feel the need because they believed that the Australians were on side.

The Australians in fact were far less cooperative than the Canadians, were also far more intrusive and at critical stages in the negotiations posed a far greater threat to British success than ever the Canadians did. They rejected most of the concessions won by Heath and were also highly critical of the British negotiating strategy. The British had hoped initially that Commonwealth countries would provide them with a list of demands and then leave it to themselves to pursue these with the six. While the Canadians concurred in that approach, the Australians certainly did not. First, the Australians considered that 'the right negotiating tactic was to move from an opening position through a long series of fall back positions until one is found which the six was willing to accept', but the British believed that there was 'a real danger in that process as it would lead to the formulation of specific proposals by the six at the lowest level at which they can reach agreement between themselves and from which they would find it difficult to move'. Better, the British considered, 'for us to put forward negotiable positions before their attitude has hardened'.[55]

While the British were prepared within that process to consult with the Commonwealth either by means of High Commissioner briefings in London, augmented by additional discussions with officials there and by on-the-spot exchanges with Commonwealth officials in Brussels, the Australians considered these to be totally inadequate. Mr McEwen complained in London in March 1962 that 'he did not feel that the Australians had been adequately consulted as the British thinking had developed over the months after the September consultations'.[56] He even chided the British (citing Dr Erhardt) of not being 'suf-

53 J.R.A. Bottomley reporting on discussions with Canadian officials, 28 March 1962, DO 159/52, PRO. 54 Duncan Sandys to Lord Amory, undated, September 1962, DO 159/44, PRO. 55 Paper by A.W. France, Commonwealth Relations Office, 10 April 1962, DO 159/58, PRO. 56 Meeting in

ficiently blunt in their presentation'.[57] Accordingly, Mr McEwen decided to pursue an independent but parallel channel of negotiations with the six, much to the chagrin of the British, especially Mr Heath. There was nothing the British could do about Australia's transmitting its own aide memoires to the six, although they could influence Australia's proposals for its own seat at the negotiating table in Brussels which as had been seen, the Canadians flatly rejected. Heath was initially shocked at the latter suggestion. In a letter to Macmillan he wrote: 'I view the possibility of participation with the greatest foreboding. I would therefore like to limit it to the minimum, that is that an Australian representative should make one appearance at official level to express his views over a whole range of problems [. . .] not as a means of getting a foot in the door so that participation can be extended to discussion on problems at other levels.'[58]

Dr Westerman, Secretary of the Australian Department of Trade, made his submission on 26 April 1962, and in it he made no concession whatsoever to the reality of either the British or the EEC situation, but beyond a polite hearing it achieved little. It had the advantage for the British in that the preparation of Westerman's 100-page address deflected Australian attention from British affairs for at least one month, thereby providing a welcome respite for Heath and his team. The Australians themselves were happy with the opportunity, and Westerman reported to McEwen that 'it was favourably received' and that the six 'learned more about the Commonwealth than from the British after eight or nine months of talking to them'.[59] However, it was never mentioned again and Heath subsequently informed Menzies that 'I feel I should qualify your reference to the favourable reaction given by the six to Dr Westerman's statement.'[60] The response to Australia's grovelling aide memoires to the EEC was equally dismissive; Australia's assertion in the September 1961 aide memoire that it had 'never sought economic aid and had been a donor of aid and that whatever arrangements can come out of the present negotiations and discussions, they would not want to become dependent on special aid' and that 'they would retain their place of dignity and value as a member of the Western countries',[61] did not impress the EEC.

Mr Macmillan was wary of calling a Commonwealth conference and Diefenbaker's persistent demand for one, heightened his apprehension. How-

London of E. Heath, J. McEwen, Dr Westerman and J. Bottomley, 21 March 1962, DO 159/57, PRO. **57** Meeting in London between E. Heath, J. McEwen, D. Sandys et al., 12 April 1962, DO 159/58, PRO. **58** E. Heath to H. Macmillan, 19 March 1962, DO 159/57, PRO. **59** Dr Westerman to J. McEwen, 28 April 1962, A 1828/274 727/4, p. 27, AA. **60** E. Heath to R.G. Menzies, 12 June 1962, A 1838/274 727/4, p. 31, AA. **61** Australian Aide Memoire to Common Market, 4 September 1961, A 1838/2 727/4, p. 12, AA.

ever, when the conference eventually did take place in September 1962, Diefenbaker was not the problem but rather Menzies and his prompter in the wings, McEwen. In a post-conference reflection, Duncan Sandys referred to the 'small impact which Diefenbaker made upon the conference' and that in the 'drafting of the crucially important communiqué he raised few difficulties and specifically stated that he would not press for the inclusion of his earlier proposal for a further meeting of prime ministers'.[62] The same could not be said for Mr Menzies. Macmillan agreed with Menzies[63] that he, Menzies, Diefenbaker and Holyoake should arrive in London some days before the scheduled opening of the conference to plan strategy for dealing with the new Commonwealth countries.[64] It is, however, doubtful if this was Macmillan's real motive; more likely it was to copper-fasten the old Commonwealth cooperation by targeting imaginary troublemakers among the new Commonwealth. Macmillan had noted in September 1962 that 'the new Commonwealth countries carry little political weight in this country' and that 'sentiment towards the Commonwealth is really centred on the old Commonwealth especially Australia and New Zealand. Their governments, if they wished, could make it almost impossible for a conservative or indeed any government to carry Britain to the Common Market'.[65]

But Macmillan did not carry Mr Menzies. Despite British promptings that the final communiqué be 'couched in general terms' and acknowledge that British 'entry into Europe was the best step we could take' to achieve 'an increase in world trade',[66] Menzies plus other Commonwealth delegates insisted on asserting 'the extent to which their interests had not so far been met in the Brussels negotiations'.[67] According to R.A. Butler, it took nearly two days and two nights to get agreement on that communiqué and that 'at one time it had appeared possible that there might have been two communiqués' which, according to Butler, 'would have been very damaging'.[68] Menzies subsequently sought to mend his bridges; on the next day, 20 September, he called on Macmillan who later informed Butler that Menzies 'was clearly trying to be as pleasant as possible and to excuse himself for not having taken a more constructive position throughout the conference'. Menzies had

62 Secretary of State for Commonwealth Relations to Lord Amory, undated, DO 159/55, PRO. 63 R.G. Menzies to H. Macmillan, 11 July 1962, PREM 11 3660, PRO. 64 H. Macmillan to R.G. Menzies, 20 July 1962, PREM 11 3660 – see also PREM 11 3360 for a note by Macmillan dated 4 November 1962 on that issue, PRO. 65 Note by H. Macmillan, 4 September 1962, PREM 11 3660, PRO. 66 R.A. Butler to H. Macmillan, 19 September 1962, PREM 11 3362, PRO. 67 Final Communiqué of Commonwealth Prime Ministers Meeting, 19 September 1962, PREM 11 3662, PRO. 68 R.A. Butler to H. Macmillan, 19 September 1962, PREM 11 3662, PRO.

explained his conduct by 'the weakness of his political position' and by the fact that 'Mr McEwen was at him all the time to take a much stronger line.'[69]

All this raises the question of why, in the light of such disruptive behaviour throughout the negotiations, Australia should still emerge as the perceived ally of Britain and the champion of toleration within the Commonwealth? First, unlike the Canadians, the Australians did not set out to be deliberately provocative. The Australian cabinet recognized that because of the attention which Australia 'had paid in Canberra, in London, in Brussels and in Washington to the British six negotiations' that it may find itself as the 'leader within the Commonwealth in Common Market affairs'. This was to be avoided at all costs. In fact the Australian cabinet had 'indicated that a development of this kind was not only being sought, but would be regarded as containing definite risks, and in particular the risk of appearing to be leading or creating opposition to Britain's entry into Europe'. The cabinet further emphasized that 'Australia had from the beginning sought to act on reasonable and constructive lines [as defined by themselves] as distinct from hostile or obstructive and it was agreed that Australia must be on guard not to be manoeuvred in fact or even in appearance into any such role'.[70] Accordingly, despite the substance and frequency of their interventions, the Australians assumed a low key in their advocacy.

Second, Menzies's standing in Britain, with politicians, the press and with the British establishment was an enormous advantage in projecting a friendly image of Australia. He was particularly close to Macmillan and while in the hurly-burley of negotiations sharp words may have been exchanged and the relationship may have been frayed at the edges, the friendship endured. In July 1962 Macmillan confided to Menzies that he 'would enormously value the chance of talking privately with you not only because of your long experience as a prime minister but because, if, I may say so, your friendship and council means so much to me'.[71] Menzies reciprocated publicly in his Australian Club dinner address at the Savoy where he referred to Macmillan as 'his old friend, this most distinguished servant of his people, whom I have known for many years and through many escapades and have been and remain great friends [. . .] The reason why we always meet as friends is that we know the story behind it all. It is the story of the Commonwealth in which he and I happen to be servants of our sovereign lady the Queen', and for the gratification of his distinguished audience he then reasserted that he was 'prime minister of a country

69 H. Macmillan to R.A. Butler, 20 September 1962, PREM 11 3663, PRO. **70** E.J. Bunting to Arthur Tange, 2 July 1962, A 1838/2 727/4, p. 32, AA. **71** H. Macmillan to R.G. Menzies, 20 July 1962, PREM 11 3660, PRO.

which is British to its boot heels [. . .] and nothing will separate the people of Australia from their allegiance to the crown'.[72]

It was understandable that Britain concluded, albeit erroneously that they could do business with Menzies, by which they meant that they could get their own way with him, failing to recognize that in the 1936 meat negotiations and also during the 1938 discussion on the revision of the Ottawa agreement, Menzies did not deliver, and certainly was not going to do so now on an issue of such paramount importance for Australia as Britain's entry into the Common Market. Menzies had another advantage in that he could project himself as the good fairy in contrast to McEwen's wicked one. In contrast to McEwen's intransigence and bluntness, Menzies projected a benign image, ever willing to understand and to accommodate if he could, but was hampered by having McEwen's shadow hovering over him. He invariably attributed the excesses of Australian demands to McEwen, over whom, he alleged, he had little influence and because of the parliamentary situation was also dependent on and even bespoken to. However, there is no evidence that Menzies either in cabinet or in private correspondence ever sought to temper McEwen's extremes, even when he (Menzies) was advised by officials in his own department to do so. Menzies fully endorsed McEwen's xenophobic and unyielding pursuit of Australian trade interests but that was never recognized, especially in Great Britain. As a result Menzies could continue to bask in his avuncular cocoon and as it was he rather than McEwen who personified Australia in British eyes, it was that image which endured. Thus while Australians pursued a much more negative policy towards British entry to the EEC they escaped the opprobrium heaped on the less active but more voluble Canadians.

In conclusion, while the entire exercise eventually proved abortive following de Gaulle's veto in January 1963, the proceedings had exposed the fragility of Commonwealth cohesion, the dominance of national interests, the absence of trust on all sides and went a long way towards dispelling the warm glow surrounding old Commonwealth country relations, allegedly so dear to Macmillan's heart. It also alerted both Australia and New Zealand to the risk of overdependence on the British market and on the Ottawa preferential system – they would have to look elsewhere and be better prepared should Britain once again make overtures to Europe. Publicly, however, they did not acknowledge that fact so that when McEwen was interviewed on radio on 31 January 1963 and asked if he was pleased that Britain had been rejected by the EEC, he answered no. The charade endured, now even more divorced from the reality.

72 Report of speech delivered 12 June 1962, A 1838/2 727/4, p. 30, AA.

11

Australian decolonization

It is usual to associate decolonization with the second half of the twentieth century and especially with countries in Asia and Africa that gained independence from European metropolitan powers. This is because decolonization is normally defined in political and constitutional terms that assume an initial conquest, the subjugation and exploitation of native people, the introduction of an alien culture, the destruction of indigenous artefacts and of defence strategies based exclusively on the needs of the metropolitan. Emancipation is usually attributed to a combination of colonial nationalism and its derivative social and structural changes, to a decline in the military and economic standing of the mother country followed by a growing indifference, even antagonism amongst the metropolitan population to empire and finally to shifts in the international balance of power. In some instances, armed rebellion is also an essential ingredient. Under any or all of these criteria, Australia would hardly qualify as a case study in decolonization.

While the Australian aborigines experienced most of the effects of colonization, they did not participate in, nor benefit from, the process and outcome of decolonization. They were conquered, they were subjugated and exploited, their artefacts were damaged and they were forced to endure an alien culture but there is no evidence of an elite emerging from amongst their ranks that could be availed of by the metropolitan in governing the continent. Nor is there evidence in the nineteenth century of aboriginal nationalism or of independence demands and when these eventually manifested themselves in the twentieth century, they were initially orchestrated by Caucasian Australians. Accordingly, those aborigines that survived the arrival of the British and Irish in Australia in 1788 were generally ignored by their new masters and were relegated to the margins of society where it was assumed, they would either expire naturally or be absorbed by the Anglo-Celt community, as underscored by section 127 of the 1900 Constitution. Ironically, then, when dealing with Australian decolonization, the indigenous people may be excluded, leaving us with the Anglo-Celts, the actual colonizers and also with the intriguing conundrum of the colonizers themselves being decolonized.

All this however assumes that a colony existed in Australia in the first place but even a cursory glance at British intentions for Botany Bay casts doubt on that proposition: for the architects of the first fleet, Botany Bay was merely an extension of the home country, an additional county, bound by the same laws as, for example, was Kent, with similar political, social and economic structures. It was seen as a settlement inhabited by settlers and not as a colony, peopled by colonists. However, within a very short time of European settlement in New South Wales, the automatic identification of the settlers with the mother country, assumed by the protagonists of the scheme, was being eroded; most of the convicts, the unwilling colonists, understandably resented their jailers; the 25% of settlers of Irish origin whose allegiances were to their homeland, had little time for Britain while most important of all, those born in the New Country, the currency men and women, did not have a physical or even an emotional attachment to the mother land. Their loyalties were with Australia and they were soon joined by the disenchanted convicts and the Irish settlers who, despite their initial longings for Ireland, were deprived in those early years of the priests that would later reinforce their identity with Ireland itself. These divergences were to be compounded by clashes between the metropolitan and the settlement on policy matters. While the disposal of convicts had been the immediate reason for taking over New South Wales, the colony's economic resources, especially the quality of its wool, were an unexpected windfall which industrialising Britain sought to exploit. This was a most divisive issue in New South Wales, with the predominantly Anglo-Saxon graziers benefitting while most other sections of society were denied a sufficient stake in the colony. In their case, all the classic colonial features of exploitation and dependency were present – they were not consulted about policy, economic development appeared to be exclusively for the benefit of the metropolitan and the privileged few in the colony while culturally, the official version was the Anglo-Saxon one that was shared only by a small colonial elite of exclusives. But even the latter's fulsome identification with Britain was short-lived. It was undermined in the 1830s when Britain sought to forge a colonial policy that would cater not only for her own industrialists but also for her surplus and impoverished population. The Rippon regulations satisfied few: the exclusives objected to British intrusion in the disposal of New South Wales land especially as there was now a hefty price to be paid and the available parcels were considered to be totally inadequate; other sections who now had access to land were similarly frustrated by the high price and also by the uneconomic nature of the available plots. James McArthur, a squatter, announced that he thought

> that the time had arrived when the long agitated emancipist question might be dropped, [when the] men of property irrespective of their social origins should combine in the face of the common enemy, Britain.[1]

The Australian Patriotic Association which had been founded in 1835 to further the popular agitation for liberal reforms in the colony and which initially comprised wealthy emancipists, free emigrants and native born, was now augmented by the presence of the exclusives. The comprehensive nature of the protest is symptomatic of the changed relationship between New South Wales and the mother land. There was no longer a coincidence of interests. Britain's overt involvement in New South Wales was considered intrusive and stultifying. The colonists believed that they had a greater appreciation than Great Britain of the needs of New South Wales and the exclusives, particularly, recognised that without their co-operation, British suzerainty in the colony was unsustainable.

Governor Gipp's personal antagonism towards the exclusives had to bow to British imperial designs – partial decolonization was the only option if only to retain a link, if now more tenuous. Political concessions were made by way of the 1847 Order in Council which granted a temporary respite for the exclusives, but more importantly, the first step towards ultimate self-government was taken in the 1842 constitution, later to be extended in 1850 and again in 1856 and of course the 1900 Federal constitution which disposed of most of the remaining ties. Thus, while Repeal of the Union was being fiercely contested in Ireland, Home Rule was nonetheless being conceded in Australia, albeit in therapeutic doses, but nonetheless without any great resistance. All of which begs the question of whether decolonization in Australia was complete with the degree of autonomy enshrined in the 1900 Constitution?

This however depends as much on the nature of the British Empire as it does on conditions in Australia. Because if concessions of independence or internal self-government were symptomatic of decolonizing, then Britain in fact was decolonizing more rapidly than she was colonizing between 1783 and 1914.[2]

1 F.K. Crowley, *A new history of Australia* (1974) p. 72. 2 John Darwin, *Britain and decolonisation* (1994), p. 4.

However, the British imperial system was far from the political or constitutional unity which the expression 'British Empire' implies, despite being viewed as a single state in international law. The fact that by the 1930s, British overseas interests were being administered by four different government departments, namely the Foreign Office, the Dominion Office, the Colonial Office and the India Office indicated a diversity of relationships that upheld British influence and prestige abroad. And that was by no means dependent on trade. In fact, before the Ottawa Agreement of 1932, Britain traded more with non-empire countries than she did with empire ones. And while critical of Macaulay's definition of the British Empire as constituting an 'imperishable Empire of our arts and our morals, our literature and our laws', its essence was, in fact, largely based on such components. It was undoubtedly strengthened by economic ties and also by the Christian creed and by sporting encounters. All contributed to providing a vehicle for British influence on the international stage. Thus while the granting of political autonomy may be considered the essential ingredient of decolonization in the late twentieth century, it was merely a necessary but not sufficient constituent in the nineteenth century.

In that sense then, Australia's informal links with Britain mattered as much to both countries as had their earlier formal ties. They embraced most areas of national life: from common parliamentary and legal systems, to cultural and sporting affinities, to defence commitments and diplomatic representation and especially to trade relations, all of which were reinvigorated by a constant stream of British migrants to Australia and Australian visitors to Britain. The *Bulletin* maintained that the Australians were Australia's 'as much full blown British subjects as the British themselves'[3] while the *London Times* went further and described Australians as 'the leaven with their fine youthfulness in our middle aged civilisation'.[4] Accordingly, the social and political order of the mother country was substantially replicated in Australia, with Australia emerging as an informal British satellite, becoming more dependent on Britain than the latter was on Australia. This was acceptable to Australians as long as they felt assured that Britain could deliver on Australian defence and trade requirements and until 1940 they had no reason to doubt Britain's sincerity or ability. The defence relationship was strengthened by the World War One experience, trade relations were reinforced and copper fastened by the Ottawa Agreement while the steady flow of migrants, dictated mainly by Australian population needs, further strengthened the bonds. Australia therefore until World War Two had no reason to doubt the wisdom of its close ties with Britain, despite its

3 Richard White, *Inventing Australia* (1981), p. 71. 4 Ibid., p. 103.

own geographic location and changes in the international balance of power. In the broad sense, Australia had only been partially decolonized by the outbreak of World War Two, if one accepts that voluntary dependency still constituted partial colonial status. The fact that Australia failed to implement the 1930 Statue of Westminster confirms that proposition.

World War Two and its aftermath was to change all of that. Now for the first time, the essentials of the British/Australian relationship were to be tested and in Australian eyes, these were found wanting. This was due not only to wartime experience and subsequent economic and demographic developments but also to the unacceptable imperial perceptions of Winston Churchill.

As in World War One, Australia immediately pledged its support for the British war effort in 1939 but in contrast to World War One, the British Prime Minister's response was to accept that undertaking as an unconditional display of loyalty – he seldom reciprocated even when Australia itself was in danger from the Japanese. He refused to resurrect the World War One Imperial War Cabinet and initially refused Dominion representation in London. Menzies reported to his cabinet that, 'Churchill had no conception of the Dominions as separate entities'[5] ignoring and belittling the Statute of Westminster. When it became clearer that Churchill was pursuing a 'Hitler first' policy and abandoning far eastern territories such as Australia to their own devices, a reappraisal of the British/Australian relationship was imperative. Curtin, Menzies' successor, grasped that nettle, declaring in December 1941 that 'Australia looks to America, free from any pangs as to our traditional links with the United Kingdom'[6] and accordingly he withdrew the Australian ninth and tenth divisions from the Middle East, refusing Churchill's request to have them deployed in the Burma campaign, and posted them to the Pacific theatre where Australia's interests were most threatened. In 1942, Australia adopted the Statute of Westminster, a vital step in legalising and asserting its own independence and a pivotal move towards full decolonization.

Similarly, in the economic sphere, Britain's gradual absorption within Europe cast doubts on her commitments to Australian trading needs. The decision to apply for membership of the European Economic Community in October 1961 was a devastating blow for Australia – it heralded the end of the Ottawa preferential trading system and Australia recognized that that would require a reorientation of its own trade policy, a fact that was reinforced by subsequent rebuffs which Britain inflicted: in May 1962, Britain acceded to the EEC demand that she end tariff preferences on manufactured goods from

5 J. Garner, *The Commonwealth Office* (1978) p. 210. 6 *Melbourne Herald*, 27 December 1941.

Australia, rejecting Australia's proposals for tariff preferential quotas. Mr Duncan Sandys' much vaunted promise of 'comparable outlets' for temperate food stuff in an enlarged common market were discarded in December 1962 and the problem was transferred to a vaguely defined World Conference on total output and sales of each commodity to be held in 1963, after Britain had been accepted into the EEC Sandys then had to write to Menzies:

> We are reluctantly forced to the conclusion that this means that there is virtually no prospect of retaining the existing Commonwealth preferences after the transitional period.[7]

These rebuffs however did not immediately alter Australia's preferences for its own society: even after the war, Australia still cherished the Anglo-Celt model. Its close shave with Japan and the dramatic drops in its own rates of natural increase during the 1930s did not auger well for Australian success in sustaining that profile unassisted. Immigrants were required and Australia's initial and exclusive preference was for the traditional Anglo-Celts. It was only when the supply proved to be inadequate that the Chiefly Labor government was forced to look elsewhere and thus began a process by which the composition of Australian society was radically changed. Between 1947 and 1951 only 41% of new settlers were British and in the 1991 census the number of United Kingdom-born in the population had fallen to 6.6%, only double the Asian component of 3.3%, with only .3% Irish-born.[8]

Thus Australia itself was no longer an exclusively Anglo-Celt derivate society. Speaking in 1995, Senator Bolkus, the then Minister for Immigration and Ethnic Affairs, referred to the

> two hundred and forty different ethnic communities scattered throughout the land. We have every language, every culture and every religious practice in the world in Australia. Not only does it permeate Australia geographically – it permeates every aspect of Australian life.

Thus even within Australia itself, the traditional dominance of the Anglo-Celt was being eroded and as a result the ties with the mother land weakened. Britain had become dispensable for Australia – which was indeed fortunate in view of Britain's own decision in 1961 to deny free entry to Britain to Australian citizens, still technically, British subjects. The children were being rejected by their mother – maybe the children had grown up.

7 Duncan Sandys to R.G. Menzies, 24 July 1962, A 1838/2727/4, p. 8, Australian Archives, Canberra. 8 *Census of Australia*, 1991.

It should therefore be apparent that Australian decolonization has been a complex process in which both the metropolitan and the colony have had varying roles to play. Two distinct stages are evident: firstly, the early nineteenth century when the initiative was taken by the colonists as they began to distance themselves from the mother country, acquiring a substantial degree of autonomy by 1900 and secondly, in the second half of the twentieth century, when the mother country appeared to be abandoning its sibling, particularly in areas of vital concern to Australia such as defence, trade and settlement, thereby creating an atmosphere of insecurity and of isolation that propelled self-reliance. However, it was a peaceful process without the residue of bitterness and of resentment found so often in other ex-colonies.

Bibliography

Bastian, J.M., D.McG. McBean and M.B. Smith (eds), *50 years of food research* (Melbourne, 1979).
Blainey, Geoffrey, *The tyranny of distance* (Melbourne, 1966).
Boland, T.P., *James Duhig* (Brisbane, 1986).
Brennan, Niall, *Dr Mannix* (London, 1965).
Browne, Noel, *Against the tide* (Dublin, 1980).
Burnley, I.H. (ed.), *Urbanization in Australia* (Cambridge, 1974).
Cain, N. and S. Glynn, 'Imperial Relations under Strain: the British-Australian debt contretemps of 1933', *Australian Economic History Review*, vol. 25, 1985, pp 39–58.
Crawford, J.G., *Australian trade policy, 1942–1966* (Canberra, 1968).
Crowley, F.K., *A new history of Australia* (Melbourne, 1974).
Darwin, John, *Britain and decolonisation* (London, 1994).
Davies, A.F. & S. Encel (eds), *Australian society* (Melbourne, 1965).
Drummond, I.M., *Imperial economic policy, 1917–39* (Toronto, 1974).
Ebsworth, Walter A., *Archbishop Mannix* (Melbourne, 1977).
Eden, A., *Facing the dictators* (London, 1962).
Encel, S., *Equality and authority* (Melbourne, 1970).
Evatt, H.V., *Australian labor leader* (Sydney, 1940).
Fanning, Ronan, *Independent Ireland* (Dublin, 1983).
Fiddes, G., *The Dominions and Colonial Offices* (London, 1926).
Fitzhardinge, L.F., *W.M.Hughes: a political biography*, vol. 2 (Melbourne, 1979).
Fukushima, T., *The Australian-Japanese trade dispute, 1936* (Tokyo, 1981).
Garner, J., *The Commonwealth Office* (London, 1978).
Greeley, Andrew, *That most distressful nation* (Chicago, 1973).
Hancock, W.K., *Survey of British Commonwealth Affairs*, vol. 2 (London, 1942).
Heuston, R.M., 'British nationality and Irish citizenship', in *International Affairs*, vol. 26, no. 1 (January 1950).
Hudson, W.J., and W. Way (eds), *Letters from a 'Secret Service Agent'* (Canberra, 1986).
Inskip, T., *Diary* (London, 1939).
Kiernan, Colm, *Daniel Mannix and Ireland* (Victoria, 1984).
Kottman, R., *Reciprocity and the North Atlantic triangle, 1932–38* (Ithaca, 1968).
La Nauze, J.A., *Alfred Deakin* (Melbourne, 1979).
MacOwen, H., *Social sketches of Australia, 1880–1975* (Melbourne, 1978).
Mansergh, N., *Survey of British Commonwealth affairs, 1931–39* (London, 1952).
McMahon, Deirdre, *Republicans and imperialists: Anglo-Irish relations in the 1930s* (Yale, 1984).
Middlemas, K. and J. Barnes, *Baldwin* (London, 1967).

Miller, J.D.B., 'The C.R.O. and the Commonwealth Relations' in *International Studies* (New Delhi), vol. 2, no. 1, Bombay (July 1960).
Miller, J.D.B., *The EEC and Australia* (Canberra, 1976).
Murphy, Frank, *Daniel Mannix: archbishop of Melbourne* (Melbourne, 1948).
O'Farrell, Patrick, *The Catholic Church in Australia* (Sydney, 1968).
O'Farrell, Patrick, *The Irish in Australia* (Sydney, 1987).
Pike, Douglas (ed.) *Australian dictionary of biography*, vol. 2 (Melbourne, 1966–2002)
Price, Charles A. (ed.), *Australian Immigration*, no. 2 (Canberra, 1970)
Richmond, W.H., 'S.M. Bruce and Australian economic policy, 1923–29', *Australian Economic History Review*, vol. 22 (1983), pp 238–57.
Santamaria, B.A., *Daniel Mannix* (Melbourne, 1984).
Scott, E., *Australia during the War,* vol. 11 (Sydney, 1936).
Shaw, A.G.L., *The story of Australia* (Sydney, 1960).
Smith, W.M., *The marketing of Australian and New Zealand primary produce* (London, 1936).
Vamplew, Wray (ed.), *Australian historical statistics* (Sydney, 1987).
White, Richard, *Inventing Australia* (Sydney, 1981).

Index